VENETO

First published in 2017
by Guardian Books, Kings Place, 90 York Way, London N1 9GU
and Faber & Faber Ltd, Bloomsbury House,
74–77 Great Russell Street, London WC1B 3DA

Designed and typeset by Anna Green at www.siulendesign.com

Printed and bound in China by C&C Offset Printing Co. Ltd

A CIP record for this book
is available from the British Library

ISBN 978-1-78335-108-4

2 4 6 8 10 9 7 5 3 1

*Recipes from
an Italian
Country Kitchen*

VENETO

VALERIA
NECCHIO

PART I

Then

*Family Recipes from the
Venetian Countryside*

14

PART II

Now

*Inspired Recipes from a
Modern Venetian Kitchen*

132

PART III

Pantry

Preserving the Seasons

248

THE ROOTS OF *VENETO*

When I say I'm Venetian, most people think I'm from Venice. Alas, that's not where I'm from. As much as I like the idea of a life among crumbling palazzi *and hazy canals, I am the sort of Venetian who grew up inland — in the countryside, the periphery. Home for me is a village — or, should I say, a cluster of houses — enveloped by miles of farmland. And though it might not stand comparison with the charms of Venice, home has always had a few good things going for it. The first, in my mind, is the food.*

For as long as I can remember, food has always played a central role in the daily life of my family, filling our days and marking our conversations. Our kitchen was constantly flooded with vegetables from grandparents' gardens — seasonal, varied, plentiful. Fresh bread was delivered daily. Locally reared meat and poultry were the centrepieces of our occasional roast dinners; these came from a farm that also happened to have walnuts in autumn, the fattest and freshest of their kind. Twice a week, seafood from the Chioggia fish market arrived at our doorstep via the itinerant fishmonger. But most importantly of all, this food was then turned into honest, home-cooked meals, shared by the four of us, twice a day, at the family table.

I grew up eating a wide array of family meals — from simple to elaborate, thrifty to bountiful — dictated, mostly, by the cook's personal repertoire and set of preferences. Within this spectrum, however, all meals and recipes shared a common theme. They were for the most part seasonal and linked to the land and its ingredients; but they were also bound to an eating and cooking culture that digs deep into the past and holds fast to local traditions and rituals. Sense of place

and timelessness are ingrained in the 'everyday' food of my *nonna*. Accustomed as she was to cooking and eating the same foods over and over again, it never occurred to her to invent or attempt something new, she just kept doing what she learnt from those who came before her, tirelessly improving her craft through practice and repetition.

Mum, on the other hand, was too curious a person to stick to the same old menu. In what we all perceived as a culinary rebellion of sorts, she pursued the new — new recipes, new flavours and new ingredients. Even though her quest remained largely within the borders of the Veneto region, it is thanks to her inquisitiveness that I had the chance to expand my tastes and, eventually, my comfort zone as a cook. At the same time, it is exactly because of her defiance of all things familiar and traditional that I became increasingly, hopelessly fascinated with the food of my origins.

––––––––––

This fascination didn't occur overnight. It took me a few years and many detours before I eventually came to it. Rather like a large painting, whose features are best admired from a distance, I had to leave that village behind and move away to truly understand the impact my heritage had on the way I shopped, cooked and ate. Living away from home — at first just two regions away, and then eventually abroad — I found myself missing the food as much as the people. This strange form of homesickness ultimately turned me into the sort of nostalgic cook who hunts down Venetian ingredients, and sustains many a conversation with family and friends about the food they grew up eating.

My sources of traditional culinary knowledge, at that point, were the above-mentioned *nonna*, who, now in her nineties, is as sharp as a pencil and still active in the kitchen, but has never bothered

writing down a single recipe in her life; and my parents, who mostly just rave about the food their *nonne* cooked for them, and yet never took an interest in scribbling down their favourite dishes. It seemed fairly clear that, if I ever wished to record the handful of heirloom recipes bound to my memory and family heritage and make sense of who I was as a person and a cook, now was time for me to do so.

A BOOK OF VENETIAN HOME COOKING

Veneto is a cookbook, but it's also a memoir of food, family and culture. In this sense, the recipes it contains are more than just a collection of regional classics: they are true family and personal favourites. These three aspects sometimes overlap, which is why, leafing through these pages, you'll come across dishes that are traditional and might therefore ring a bell: *risi e bisi*, *bigoi in salsa*, *tiramisù* etc. However, you'll also stumble upon a few modern classics, or recipes that are not typical of the Veneto but that for a variety of reasons came to be part of the family repertoire. *Gnocchetti al pesto* and *sbrisolona* are just two examples of these carefully chosen intrusions.

Venetian countryside home cooking — the backbone of this book — is still relatively untrodden territory. Very few cookery authors have ventured beyond Venice's glistening water walls, and this has left a huge chunk of the region undocumented, unheard of, uncelebrated. With *Veneto*, I wanted to shift the main focus away from Venice and capture a piece of the often-overlooked hinterland through its food. Of course, Venice has not been left out of the picture, quite the opposite: as the city where most of Veneto's iconic dishes have been forged, Venice continues to play a crucial role in the gastronomic geography of the area. The hefty handful of *ricette veneziane* in this book (like *baccalà mantecato*, *sarde in saor* and *mezzo uovo con l'acciuga*) is a testament to the city's strong cultural and culinary pull on the region, my family and myself.

––––––––––

The recipes, a hundred in total, are divided between three sections.

The first section, **Then**, is a collection of time-honoured family recipes from the generations past, as well as some iconic Venetian dishes that marked my upbringing. The food in this section is hearty, old-school and substantial, while maintaining a seasonal soul. The recipes take you through a classic five-course Italian meal, starting with *antipasti* and nibbles; followed by *primi* (a first course of soup, pasta or rice); *secondi* (fish and meat); *contorni* (sides); and closing with *dolci* and baked treats. To stay true to the way we refer to them at home, some of the dishes in this section are listed in the Venetian dialect.

The second part, **Now**, gathers recipes and stories as collected while living away from home. The recipes in this section draw inspiration from a wider range of influences and have a more modern twist, but remain deeply bound to a Venetian way of cooking that follows the seasons and is centred around specific flavours and ingredients. Again this section works through the five courses.

This divide between **Then** and **Now** isn't purely practical. Rather, it represents the way I cook and eat, always oscillating between the old and the new, past and present, tradition and invention.

Finally, a shorter section called **Pantry** celebrates the cherished ritual of preserving seasonal produce through drying, pickling and jamming. Here, I have included ten of my favourite sweet and savoury preparations from across the seasons.

I hope you'll find something you like; something you'd cook for yourself on any given night, or something you'd make to impress your mum or your friends. And then, I hope you'll find something you'll want to cook again and again, and will eventually make yours, moulding the recipe to your own tastes as you become familiar with it. That is, in my mind, the best part about home cooking.

––––––––––

MY VENETIAN PANTRY

Below is a list of ingredients that I have in my kitchen most of the time (save some seasonal variations), and that I would suggest you keep in mind whenever the mood for a Venetian-inspired meal takes you. Many of these you may already have in your fridge and kitchen cupboards; others you should be able to source from good delis and grocers, as well as online suppliers.

STORECUPBOARD

Almonds — whole and blanched
Anchovies — salted or in olive oil
Aperol (or Campari)
Linguine
Moscato Passito (Italian dessert wine)
Olive oil — Italian extra virgin
  (see Note on Ingredients)
Pine nuts
Polenta (cornmeal)
Prosecco
Raisins
Risotto rice — Vialone Nano and Carnaroli
Sea salt — fine-grain and flaky
Spaghetti — thin and thick
Tomatoes — passata or sauce; peeled & tinned; purée
Wheat flour — unbleached and stone-milled
Wine vinegar (see Note on Ingredients)

FRUIT AND VEGETABLES

Asparagus — white and green
Borlotti beans — fresh and dried
Figs
Garlic
Lemons — unwaxed
Olives
Onions
Peas — fresh and frozen
Pomegranate
Potatoes
Pumpkin
Radicchio
Tomatoes
Wild mushrooms

MEAT AND FISH

Baccalà — stockfish and salted cod
Game — guinea fowl, wild rabbit, quails
Lard — fresh and salt-cured *lardo*
Mackerel
Octopus
Pork — fresh and cured (salame,
  sopressa, prosciutto)
Poultry
Sardines — fresh and salted
Sea bream and sea bass
Shellfish — clams, mussels, prawns,
  razor clams, scampi, shrimp
Squid and cuttlefish

HERBS AND SPICES

Basil
Bay leaves
Black peppercorns
Cinnamon — ground
Parsley — flat-leaf

FRIDGE

Butter — unsalted
Eggs — free-range and/or organic
  (see Note on Ingredients)
Grana Padano and Parmigiano Reggiano
  (see Note on Ingredients)
Mascarpone
Milk — whole
Ricotta

A NOTE ON INGREDIENTS

SALT: The recipes in this book have been tested using sea salt only — never table salt. I use coarse sea salt for salting water; flakey sea salt (such as Maldon) for certain vegetable or meat dishes; and fine-grain sea salt for everything else. That said, every type and every brand holds a different degree of 'saltiness', which is why I always recommend you taste the food and adjust according to your liking.

OILS: Although not a quintessentially Venetian ingredient, olive oil is now commonly used in traditional as much as in modern cooking. Personally, I use olive oil for both dressing and cooking — though I prefer sunflower oil for deep-frying. For stir-frying, braising and baking, my preference is for a milder variety of extra virgin olive oil; whereas for cold dressing and finishing, I keep a couple of more 'special' oils on hand that have different degrees of piquancy and body, and interchange them depending on the dish.

VINEGARS: Venetians use a lot of vinegar in their cooking, mostly to sharpen the edges of a dish or cut the oiliness, and it's almost always wine vinegar — white mostly, sometimes red. Balsamic vinegar, originally from the neighbouring region of Emilia Romagna, is now widely used in salad dressings and to finish meat dishes, though you'll seldom see it coming up in this book.

EGGS: The eggs I use weigh around 60g — and so fall into the medium category in the UK (and into the large in the US). Larger eggs are likely to increase baking times and compromise the texture of your baked goods. In all cases, opt for free-range, organic eggs wherever possible.

PASTA: Whenever I mention a type of pasta in the ingredient list, I normally mean the dried kind, unless otherwise stated. Use whichever brand you like (we all have our favourites), but I recommend bronze-die pasta that is made with 100% durum wheat (semolina) — both signs of greater quality.

BREADCRUMBS: The type of breadcrumbs Italians (including myself) use is called *pangrattato*, which is made from pulverised dried bread (nothing else). These are the sorts of breadcrumbs I call for in this book. I recommend making your own, or else buying Italian-style fine breadcrumbs. Panko and flaky breadcrumbs, on the other hand, won't give you the same results.

PARMIGIANO REGGIANO & GRANA PADANO: These two crumbly, Italian grating cheeses that look basically the same are often used interchangeably. I tend to keep both, and use Grana Padano for cooking and grating, and 24-month Parmigiano for shaving on dishes and serving as a snack, alongside prosecco, at the start of a meal.

USEFUL UTENSILS

My kitchen is itinerant. In the past five years I have lived in several different flats, in Italy, England and Australia, and set up home in kitchens of all sizes and guises. Conscious and accepting of my nomadic life, I had to learn to go without heavy kitchen equipment and go back to a way of cooking akin to, funnily enough, Grandma's.

That said, I still hold onto a small kitchen arsenal that comes with me wherever I go, because it has never failed to make my cooking life better and, most importantly, easier. These are the type of utensils I call for most often in this book.

FOOD MILL OR *MOULI*: For making tomato sauce, fruit jelly and jam, or for puréeing beans and vegetables.

THERMOMETERS: I keep one for high temperatures, useful when deep-frying; one for jams, to check the setting point; and one for the oven, to make sure it is heating to the right temperature. An instant digital thermometer for meat is also handy.

KITCHEN SCALE: I use a scale for everything, but especially for baking, or anything that requires extra precision. Weight measurements will always be more accurate than their volume counterparts, particularly in regards to dry ingredients. For this reason, I would encourage you to invest in a flat digital scale: it's light, handy (you can tare it as you add ingredients), and it hardly takes up any space.

HAND-HELD STICK BLENDER: Optional, but handy when making stock, creamy soup, pesto and mayonnaise.

ELECTRIC WHISK: To whip up eggs for just about anything, from zabaglione to mascarpone cream for *tiramisù*.

SPICE GRINDER: To grind nuts and grains into fresh flour.

KNIVES: A quality all-purpose chef's knife, plus a bread knife and a smaller paring knife is all I need on most days; these three form a good starter kit.

The recipes in this section bridge three generations of family cooks. Some are recipes my grandparents used to make on their farm. Others are engrained in my parents' memories and have been passed down to me by means of much culinary trial and error, and collective recollection. Others again have a more recent history, and are linked to the years I lived at home. What holds them all together is their rooted, regional and established spirit and their unfussy way of being. I hope you enjoy the stories that come with them as well.

PART I
Then

Family Recipes from the
Venetian Countryside

Surrounded by sweeps of corn, soy and sugar beets, the scenery of the Venetian inland might not seduce you at first sight. The landscape today is flat, dim and rural. And yet, it was once less daunting, beautiful even, in its own un-showy way. Stretching between rivers and canals, the land was vast, bountiful and fertile. Where now there is mere monoculture, miles and miles of ever-changing farmland existed — vineyards, fruit orchards, poplar forests, vegetable patches and wheat fields.

The abandoned farmhouses that punctuate today's landscape — nothing more than a pile of shrubbery and shaky walls — were once active centres of food production and consumption. Away from the rich, commercial cities of Venice and Padua, these farms were the throbbing hearts of the local *cucina povera*. It was here that the region's humble yet time-honoured culinary traditions were sustained through the daily rituals of creating meals out of simple, seasonal, local ingredients.

It is on farms like these that my grandparents spent their hard-working lives — growing their own vegetables, milling corn and wheat, baking their own bread, raising a few animals and making wine. It sounds idyllic now, but the reality was less rosy. In a region where many farmers starved and were often forced to leave in search of a better future, my grandparents considered themselves lucky to put food on the table — and they never took food for granted. Their meals were intrinsically thrifty and uncomplicated, often repetitive, and yet also filled with the intangible knowledge that they inherited from those in their family who came before them.

Born in the 1950s, my parents lived in a time of transition. They belong to the generation that escaped from this seemingly bucolic but largely unpractical lifestyle in favour of a more modern, comfortable way of living — namely, a house with central heating, a proper kitchen instead of a wood-fire stove, and a bathroom. They left their farms and moved to town with their families when they were teenagers. Of course, they were glad they did, but they have since nurtured a subtle yearning for the life and food of their youth. They used to have animals. They fished. They picked fruits from their own trees and foraged for wild herbs. The food they grew up eating was more immediate, more palpable. It had more flavour — or so they say.

As for me, I didn't grow up on a farm, but I did live for the best part of my life in the tiny village of my grandparents, rooted in that culture that was part ancient, deeply rural, and intrinsically Venetian. Food, like any aspect of local culture, was a mixture of old and new, a mishmash of tradition and modernity, depending largely on who was on duty at the stove. Mum's modern Venetian-fusion everyday cuisine was somewhat balanced by the strictly old-school Sunday lunches we all enjoyed at Grandma's. And even though there is a clear difference between the two styles, it all belongs, in my mind, to the realm of the past — classic and timeless.

———

BACCALÀ MANTECATO
Dried Cod Mousse

SCHIE FRITE
Fried Grey Shrimp

SARDE IN SAOR
Fried Marinated Sardines with Onions

OVI E SPARASI
White Asparagus & Boiled Eggs

FRITAJA DE ERBE
Frittata with Wild Herbs

AFFETTATI MISTI
Cured Meats

CROSTINI DE POENTA COL LARDO
Grilled Polenta 'Crostini' with Lardo

POENTA E FUNGHI
Polenta with Wild Mushrooms & Grana

MARONI ROSTI
Roasted Chestnuts

ANTIPASTI

Dried Cod Mousse

SERVES 6

600g | 1lb 5oz stockfish
  (ideally Ragno quality —
  see Note overleaf)
1 garlic clove, grated
180ml | ¾ cup extra virgin
  olive oil, or as needed
60ml | ¼ cup whole milk
2 tablespoons finely chopped
  flat-leaf parsley (optional)
Fine-grain sea salt and freshly
  ground black pepper, to taste

* Venetians use the word
baccalà to mean dried cod
(stockfish). However, in the
rest of Italy the word is used
to describe salted cod. Bear
this in mind when cooking
a Venetian recipe calling for
baccalà.

This recipe embodies the spirit of the book: it's classic and yet modern, and displays many of the main traits of the food of Veneto.

Dried cod (baccalà*) is the frontman of Venetian cuisine. It plays various roles, from quick snack to substantial main dish, and appears in many guises on the menus of most local eateries. Dried cod was introduced to Veneto by means of a group of Venetian merchants trading with Norway; they found that the large Norwegian cod, cured by the cold and dry Arctic wind, made for a great import — one that would last a long time without spoiling. Back in Venice, locals welcomed it thanks to its durable and versatile nature, and eventually elevated it to the rank of key ingredient in the regional repertoire.

In the realm of baccalà mantecato recipes, personal preferences and additions are accepted: a drop of milk (or even cream), a handful of parsley, grated garlic or a bit of black pepper all might play a part. Personally, I like adding milk to my baccalà as I find that it blunts the edges of the dish (in a good way) and fades the fishy flavour ever so slightly. It also contributes to a whiter, fluffier result — the ultimate aim. A hint of black pepper goes in, and some garlic, but no parsley. That said, these are my preferences — I encourage you to experiment, taste and adjust until you find your happy place. Make this recipe a starting point.

CONTINUED OVERLEAF

Note: Ragno is the top quality stockfish; use where possible. If you can't find stockfish, substitute salted cod and proceed as follows: skip the initial pounding and go straight to the soaking; drain and boil the fish as it is and then discard the bones and skin after cooking; continue with the creaming and whipping as described in the recipe.

On a large wooden board, pound the fish with a meat pounder (or a hammer) until tenderised, about 15 minutes. Cut it into pieces small enough to fit comfortably in your largest bowl, cover with cold water and place in the fridge to soak. Change the water twice a day for the following 48 hours.

When ready to make the *baccalà*, drain the cod and rinse it well. Open the pieces and remove skin, bones and any guts. Place the flesh in a pan and cover with cold water. Bring to the boil and then cook for about 20 minutes, or until the fish feels very tender when pierced with a fork and falls apart easily. Remove from the heat and drain. Shred the flesh with a fork and transfer to a deep bowl or pan. Add the grated garlic and stir through.

Working with a sturdy whisk or a wooden spoon in one hand, and the oil in the other, start pouring in the oil in a thin stream, whisking and whipping energetically all the while to incorporate it. Keep going for about 15 minutes, until the fish looks airy and mousse-like. At this point, add the milk and parsley, if using, and whisk some more to incorporate, then taste and season.

Transfer the *baccalà* to a container, cover and let it reach room temperature before placing in the fridge to cool for at least 1 hour. Serve slightly chilled or at room temperature, with crostini or grilled polenta.

Fried Grey Shrimp

SERVES 4–6

600g | 1lb 5oz small grey
  shrimp (any kind that can
  be eaten whole, without
  being shelled)
30g | ¼ cup plain flour, sifted
Sunflower oil, for frying
1 egg, lightly beaten
Fine-grain sea salt

For the polenta (optional):
1.2 litres | 5 cups water
10g | 2 teaspoons fine-grain
  sea salt
200g | 1¼ cup polenta
  (preferably not instant —
  see Note overleaf)

One of Grandma's many food weaknesses is fritaja coe schie, *an omelette studded with fried grey shrimp* (schie *or* schille) *that are typical of the Venetian lagoon. She makes it every Wednesday, the day the fishmonger from the nearby seaside town of Chioggia passes through our village. Sitting by the window, she listens out for the honking of the fishmonger's Ape three-wheeler; at the first* beep beep, *she springs up from the chair and down the stairs, ready for some fruitful shrimp shopping.*

Fried and generously salted, the tiny shrimp are bound by a couple of eggs from her chicken coop, and then re-fried into an omelette of sorts. The final result — crisp, salty and creamy all at once — is nothing short of spectacular.

More recently, Mum has reinvented the traditional recipe by cutting the egg content to a minimum, so as to let the shrimp be the star of the show. I'm sharing her recipe here, as I like it best (I've told Grandma). A bed of soft polenta is mandatory according to Mum, so I've included the recipe for polenta too. But if you'd rather just have the fried shrimp, a nice way to serve these is in paper cones, street food style — a winning solution for a standing aperitivo.

Rinse the shrimp in cold running water and pat them dry. Spoon the flour into a plastic bag and add the shrimp. Hold the bag tightly closed and shake gently so that the flour coats the shrimp. Tumble the shrimp into a sieve and shake off any excess flour. Set aside.

CONTINUED OVERLEAF

Note: Venetians often pair seafood with a kind of white polenta. The Biancoperla variety is rare but worth seeking out, though any fine, non-instant polenta is good all the same. If using instant polenta, follow the instructions on the package, but increase the dose of water as needed to keep the density in check.

Fill two-thirds of a medium, high-sided frying pan with sunflower oil. Place it over a medium-high heat, and wait until it reaches 180°C | 350°F, which you can test with a thermometer or by inserting the handle of a wooden spoon in the oil; when small but fierce bubbles form around the handle, it's ready. Slip in a batch of shrimp (about one-third of the total) and fry until you see them changing colour — this won't take more than a couple of minutes. Drain with a slotted spoon and transfer to a large plate covered with kitchen paper. Salt generously and keep warm. Repeat in batches.

Place a separate frying pan over a medium heat. Add the fried *schie* and then the egg. Move them around with a wooden spoon until the egg is set but still creamy, and the shrimp look bound by a pale creamy coating. Remove from the heat, transfer to a plate and keep warm.

For the polenta, bring the water to a rolling boil in a medium pan. Add the salt and allow it to dissolve, then reduce the heat to a simmer. Use a whisk to create a vortex in the water and gradually add the polenta, whisking all the while to prevent lumps from forming. Once all the polenta is added, swap the whisk for a wooden spoon and start stirring. Cook the polenta for 40–45 minutes, stirring all the while, until it has lost its grainy texture. Since the goal is to obtain a loose polenta, keep the thickness in check by adding a little hot water when needed.

Serve as a bed for the shrimp as soon as it's ready, to avoid further thickening.

Fried Marinated Sardines with Onions

SERVES 4–6

1kg | 2lb 3oz medium-sized
    sardines, gutted and scaled,
    heads removed
40g | ⅓ cup plain flour, sifted
Sunflower oil, for frying
1kg | 2lb 3oz white onions,
    thinly sliced
160ml | ⅔ cup white wine
    vinegar
5g | 1 teaspoon caster sugar
Fine-grain sea salt and freshly
    ground black pepper, to taste

Marinating fried foods in vinegar, onions and other sweet and sour elements is an ancient practice in Venetian cuisine, which holds the name of saor *(literally, 'flavour'). Venetians are known for being fond of the combination of sweet and acidic, or* dolsegarbo, *most notably with fish. Today, the practice has spread to other foods, too, from shellfish to vegetables such as aubergine and pumpkin (see page 150), giving way to a whole new range of sweet and sour delights.*

Although it's now a year-round presence on Venetian menus, sarde in saor *remains a summer starter. Served cold, its distinctive acidity makes it pleasant even in the warmest of weathers. Each household has a preferred way of preparing this dish: with white wine or just vinegar; with a touch of cinnamon; with pine nuts and raisins. Here I've shared the version we make at home, with sweet white onions (a must!) and, of course, sardines; but with otherwise not much adornment.*

Rinse the sardines in cold water. Place them in a colander in the sink and let them drain for half an hour. Run them under cold water once more and then pat dry with kitchen paper.

Place the flour in a large bowl, add the sardines and toss to dust evenly; shake off any excess. Fill two-thirds of a medium, high-sided frying pan with sunflower oil. Place it over a medium-high heat, and wait until it reaches 180°C | 350°F, which you can test with a thermometer or by inserting the handle of a wooden spoon in the oil (see previous recipe). Slip in a batch of sardines (6–8, depending on size). Fry for a couple of minutes each side, or until golden brown outside and opaque inside. Drain and transfer to a plate covered with kitchen paper. Salt generously. Carry on in batches, salting as you go.

CONTINUED OVERLEAF

Discard the oil with the exception of a very thin film — just enough to coat the bottom of the frying pan. Set this back over a medium heat, add the onions and sweat gently until very soft, stirring often so they don't brown. Next, whisk the vinegar with the sugar and pour it in. Reduce the liquid to about half its volume, remove from the heat, taste and season with salt and pepper.

Arrange a layer of sardines in a large glass bowl. Cover with a layer of white onions and then repeat in layers until you have finished all the ingredients, finishing with onions. Pour any remaining cooking liquid on top and leave to cool to room temperature before wrapping in cling film and setting in the fridge to marinate for 24 hours. Serve at room temperature.

White Asparagus & Boiled Eggs

SERVES 4

24 white asparagus spears
8 eggs
Extra virgin olive oil
White wine vinegar
Fine-grain sea salt and freshly
    ground black pepper, to taste

VARIATION:

If you can't find white
asparagus, try the dish with
some fat, outdoor-grown
green asparagus.

Ovi e sparasi is a more a ritual than a dish. It entails consuming copious amounts of white asparagus by dipping them in a sauce of hard-boiled eggs mashed with olive oil, salt, pepper and vinegar. You dip and eat, dip and eat and before you know it, you're so full that there's no room left; but you'll have just had one the best foods spring has to offer.

White asparagus is a rather precious treat, so it's worth choosing carefully. In Veneto, the best come from Bassano del Grappa: tender top to bottom, and with a shiny porcelain complexion, their distinct sweetness set them in a league of their own. They tend to be quite thick, too, which is considered a prized feature. Opt for spears that appear turgid but not dry, and ensure that their tips are undamaged.

Trim the bottom of the asparagus so that they are roughly the same length. Peel off any stringy, woody part using a vegetable peeler. Rinse them thoroughly under cold running water, pat dry and divide into 3 bundles. Tie each bundle with some food-safe string or muslin.

Place the asparagus in a tall pan, ensuring that they fit upright. Add enough water so that only the tips are uncovered. Take the asparagus out. Bring the water to the boil, add 1 teaspoon of salt, allow it to dissolve, then add the asparagus bundles, tips up. Boil for 15–30 minutes (depending on thickness), or until the asparagus feel tender when pierced with a knife. Drain with a slotted spoon, untie and arrange on a serving plate.

Meanwhile, put the eggs in a pan and cover with water. Place over a medium heat and bring to the boil. As soon as the water boils, remove from the heat and cover with a lid. Leave the eggs in the water for 10 minutes, then drain and peel. Cut them in half and arrange around the asparagus.

For the seasoning, reach for salt, black pepper, olive oil and vinegar and make a sort of saucy puddle in a corner of your plate (about 4:1 oil to vinegar). Place half an egg over the puddle and press it down decisively using the back of a fork, until you have something resembling a *gribiche*, which you'll use to dip your asparagus into.

Frittata with Wild Herbs

SERVES 6

45ml | 3 tablespoons extra
   virgin olive oil
2 garlic cloves
700g | 1½lb mixed wild
   leaves and shoots (young
   dandelion leaves, poppy
   leaves, bladder campion,
   young nettles, wild hop
   shoots, mallow leaves),
   washed, drained, trimmed
   and roughly chopped
8 eggs
50g | 1¾oz Grana Padano,
   grated
60ml | ¼ cup whole milk
30g | 2 tablespoons unsalted
   butter
Fine-grain sea salt and freshly
   ground black pepper, to taste

Note: This recipe is open to
local and seasonal variations.
I list wild herbs and shoots
commonly found in Veneto in
the spring, though you should
use whichever edible wild
greens you can get your hands
on. Opt for young and tender
shoots and leaves; if they
seem too tough, blanch in
salted water before stir-frying.
For dandelion and nettle, in
particular, pick plants that
haven't gone to flower.

Twenty-fifth April marks the end of World War II in Italy. On the same date, Venetians also observe Saint Mark's Day, patron of the city, an event that is very much part of the foundations of Venice. In the city, celebrations used to include, among other things, a bowl of risi e bisi *(see page 53), while in the countryside people would generally gather in grassy fields or along riverbanks for a humble spring banquet of wild herb frittata, wine, salame and other bucolic brilliance.*

This frittata picnic has become a nostalgic activity these days. I haven't done it in a while, but I can still taste the bread, toasted on the camping stove, too often on the wrong side of charred. And I can taste the frittata, bitter and yet somehow addictive — eggs laced with cheese and dandelion leaves and vaguely aromatic hop shoots, the herbs all picked right then and there at the picnic site, the eggs oozing and buttery. It all had a glow of ancestry, real and down-to-earth, that made that simple frittata with bread one of the most awaited meals of the year.

Heat the oil with the garlic in a large frying pan. Add the greens and fry over a medium-low heat, stirring often, until soft and wilted, about 10 minutes. Season with salt and pepper. Remove from the heat, discard the garlic, squeeze the greens to remove any excess liquid and chop roughly.

In a large bowl, combine the eggs, grated Grana, milk and seasoning and whisk until barely combined. Stir in the greens and fold through.

In a medium non-stick frying pan, melt the butter over a low heat. When foaming, add the egg mixture and cover with a lid. Allow it to cook for about 7 minutes, after which you should be able to lift the bottom with a spatula and the top should be sufficiently set. Slide the frittata onto a plate, place the skillet on top (careful, it's hot!) and turn everything upside-down so that the top is now at the bottom.

Finish cooking the frittata for a further 4–5 minutes. Remove from the heat and leave to rest, covered, for about 5 minutes, then transfer to a plate, slice and serve. This is good at room temperature, too.

Cured Meats

If there's a savoury snack-cum-starter that is typical of the Venetian countryside, it has to be cured meats. Walk into any osteria, agriturismo, food festival or even household, and salame will be served to you — along with wine and pan biscotto (the local crunchy bread). Venetians love their cured meats to an irrational extent, and consume them in copious amounts.

I wish I could share Grandpa's recipe for making salame. I never managed to ask him, and the curing tradition was abandoned long before I was born. I also wish I could share the experience of sleeping in the camera dei salami (the bedroom doubled as curing facility because of its favourable ventilation and mould concentration) and tell you all about the lovely musty smell I'm so fond of.

Instead, I'm sharing a few suggestions to recreate the look of a typical Venetian charcuterie board. Some types of meat might be a bit harder to find so please don't go mad in the quest; think of this as a piece of advice, which you can take or ignore, and then do as you please. Complete your board with grissini (breadsticks) and other forms of crunchy and/or fresh bread and then pair it all with a bone-dry Lambrusco or a fruity red (perhaps a Merlot from the Colli Euganei).

SOPRESSA (or *soppressa*) Think large salame made with pork meat and fat, spiced with salt and pepper and, typically, a hefty dose of raw garlic. Texture-wise, it is not far from *finocchiona* — the best specimens show a bit of crumbliness and are good sliced thickly. Some of the best *sopresse* come from Vicenza and have the DOP certification, though other very good ones can be found in the Treviso area as well as in the province of Padua.

PANCETTA Sliced thinly, pancetta is a fantastic product — a melting delight where meat and fat, sweet, savoury and spice are in perfect balance — to be enjoyed as part of an antipasti board. Aside from the common flat (*tesa*) and rolled (*arrotolata*) pancetta, from Vicenza come the prized *pancetta col tocco* (a piece of pork fillet rolled with the belly) and the *pancetta con l'ossocollo* (pork neck meat), all worth seeking out.

LARDO Salt-cured flat *lardo* is something Tuscans are known for, but Venetians, particularly those living in the countryside, have a long-held tradition of making this product at home. Great-Grandma Maria used to make it and then use it as flavouring for soups and stews. These days, *lardo* is an excellent complement to a salame board, too, especially when thinly sliced and left to melt on a piece of hot toast (or polenta, see page 36).

SALAME There are so many varieties of salame made in Veneto that I'd be hard-pressed to make a comprehensive list. My advice here would be to go to your favourite Italian deli, ask for advice, have a taste of everything and then pick according to your preference. Buy a whole piece and slice it at home to make the most of its flavour and texture. Pre-sliced salame tends to dry out too quickly.

PROSCIUTTO VENETO BERICO-EUGANEO This is a cured ham from the hills of Padua and Vicenza, and an excellent (DOP) local alternative to Prosciutto di Parma. Often enjoyed *tagliato al coltello* (knife-carved), it's delightful on a charcuterie platter, but can also be served with a handful of jammy figs (see page 149) or a ripe local melon.

Grilled Polenta 'Crostini' with Lardo

SERVES 4–6

100g | 3½oz thinly sliced
    cured lardo
1 teaspoon very finely
    chopped rosemary leaves

For the polenta:
1.2 litres | 5 cups water
10g | 2 teaspoons fine-grain
    sea salt
300g | scant 2 cups polenta
(preferably not instant —
    see Note below)

Note: You can of course use
instant polenta. Follow the
instructions on the package,
ensuring that your polenta
turns out on the thick side
so that it can be sliced and
grilled. If in a hurry, you
can also use ready-made
packaged polenta, which
is perfect for grilling.
Alternatively, sliced and
toasted bread works, too.

Polenta is the staple crop of the region. Well beyond the turn of the last century, many Venetian farming families didn't have anything else to eat; they ate polenta every day, at every meal. Thankfully things have changed, though polenta remains the iconic accompaniment to a number of traditional dishes, acting either as the medium to collect the juices of stews and braises, or as the starchy sidekick to grilled meats and fishes.

In this recipe, polenta replaces bread as the vehicle for cured meats, in this case lardo. *Dressed like a crostino, grilled polenta — charred, warm, topped with glistening slices of* lardo *melting away — makes for a wonderful cold-weather starter, easy enough to enjoy at a family meal, but also novel enough to impress a table of guests.*

For instructions on making the polenta, see page 26. Ensure the texture is not too loose by using the amount of water listed above — you want the polenta to be thick and just starting to detach from the sides of the pan. Once ready, tumble the polenta onto a large round or square wooden board and leave to cool and set completely.

To cut the polenta, use a sharp knife with the blade slightly wet, or better still, a piece of cotton thread. Slice it in one direction (the slices should be about 4cm | 1½ inches wide) and then cut these into small squares of roughly the same size.

Place a griddle pan over a medium-high heat. When very hot, add the polenta pieces and grill them for about 5 minutes each side, or until you see dark marks forming on the surface. Remove them from the heat and transfer to a serving platter. Top each with half a slice of *lardo*, allow it to melt ever so slightly (after a couple of minutes you'll see it go slightly transparent), and serve with a sprinkle of chopped rosemary.

Polenta with Wild Mushrooms & Grana

SERVES 4

For the mushrooms:

400g | 14oz wild mushrooms

30g | 2 tablespoons unsalted butter

1 garlic clove, whole but lightly crushed

30ml | 2 tablespoons dry white wine

2 tablespoons very finely chopped flat-leaf parsley leaves

Fine-grain sea salt and freshly ground black pepper, to taste

For the polenta:

1.5 litres | 6¼ cups water

10g | 2 teaspoons fine-grain sea salt

250g | heaped 1½ cups polenta (preferably not instant — see Note on page 26)

30g | 2 tablespoons unsalted butter

100g | 3½oz Grana Padano, grated

Wild mushrooms that grow in the lush hills of the Parco dei Colli Euganei are particularly prized: from ginger girolles to svelte chanterelles, from fat porcini (ceps) to crowded chiodini *(honey mushrooms), gatherers and gourmands have room to go wild. As soon as they come into season in late summer, they become the undisputed stars of markets and restaurant menus.*

We have never been mushroom hunters in my family — we save our talents for wild herbs — but we have never failed to secure our share at the market. Mum's first instinct would be to lace them in a steamy bowl of risotto. At times, however, she varies her offering by turning them into a topping for cheesy polenta.

The polenta in question has a specific texture: neither loose (the sort you'd serve with seafood, see page 26) nor thick (the slicing and grilling kind, see page 36), but somewhere in between the two. In this case the polenta has a flavour of its own, too — thanks to the addition of butter and Grana — though not nearly enough to overshadow the earthiness of the mushrooms.

Trim the roots off the mushrooms and clean off any dirt, moss or debris using a clean damp cloth. Heat the butter in a medium frying pan and when foaming, add the garlic. Let it infuse the butter for a couple of minutes, then add the mushrooms. Increase the heat to high and let them absorb the butter. Now, pour in the wine and allow it to evaporate. Continue to cook for 4–5 minutes, stirring often, until the liquid they released has reduced. Season with salt and pepper. Remove from the heat, discard the garlic and top with the parsley. Set aside, but keep warm.

For instructions on making the polenta, see page 26. When the polenta is ready (creamy but not too dense), stir in the butter and grated Grana until melted. Serve the polenta in bowls, topped with the mushrooms.

Roasted Chestnuts

SERVES 4

700g | 1½lb fresh chestnuts

There are three signs that signal the start of autumn in my mind: the scent of burnt wood on your clothes; fading daylight; and the cheerful cracking of chestnuts roasting over an open flame. Walk through an Italian town in autumn and, on the corner of a main road or piazza, you'll likely stumble upon a street vendor who is bent over an iron brazier, manoeuvring a cast-iron skillet filled with crackling caldarroste.

We didn't have a caldarroste *man in the village where I grew up, so we had to roast them at home. Take a day in November. It's 5pm, the sun has set, it's too early to think about dinner, but lunch has become a fading memory. That's exactly when Dad would pull out the blackened skillet and say, 'I bought some chestnuts, fancy a snack?'*

Using a small, sharp knife, slash the curved side of the nut. Then, cook the nuts following either method described below.

METHOD 1: GAS HOB OR FIREPLACE

Working in batches, arrange the nuts in a single layer in a large cast-iron skillet, ideally a chestnut pan with holes. If working on a gas stove, place the skillet over the largest burner and set the heat to medium-high. Pan-roast the chestnuts for 8–10 minutes, turning frequently and checking that the slash has opened and they are tender all the way through before removing them from the heat. If, on the other hand, you're working with a fireplace, set a rack over the open flame and cook them for a couple of minutes per side (again, the exact time will depend on the size of the nuts). Once ready, transfer the chestnuts to a paper bag. Leave to cool for about 10 minutes, then peel and eat.

METHOD 2: OVEN

Preheat the oven to 200°C | 390°F | gas mark 6. Place the chestnuts, scored side up, on a baking tray lined with parchment. Bake for about 30 minutes, or until opened and tender all the way through. Remove from the oven and place in a paper bag. Leave to cool for about 10 minutes, then peel and eat.

MINESTRONE
Chunky Vegetable & Bean Soup

MENESTRA DE FASOI
Bean & Pasta Soup

RISOTTO DE BRUSCANDOLI
Wild Hop Risotto

RISI E BISI
Rice & Pea Soup

RISI E SUCA
Rice & Pumpkin Soup

RISOTTO DE FEGADINI
Chicken Liver Risotto

TAIADELE COL CONEJO
Tagliatelle with Rabbit Ragù

BIGOI COL RAGÙ DE ANARA
Bigoli with Duck Ragù

BIGOI IN SALSA
Bigoli with Anchovies & Onions

PRIMI

Chunky Vegetable & Bean Soup

SERVES 4

300g | 10½oz dried borlotti
beans (or other white bean
of your choice), soaked
overnight
30ml | 2 tablespoons extra
virgin olive oil, plus more
for serving
1 golden onion, finely chopped
2 carrots, peeled and diced
2 celery sticks, trimmed and
finely chopped
300g | 10½oz dry-fleshed
pumpkin, peeled and cubed
1 waxy potato (300g | 10½oz),
peeled and cubed
100g | 3½oz pearl barley
60g | 2oz Parmesan rind, cut
into small cubes
2 tablespoons finely chopped
flat-leaf parsley leaves
Fine-grain sea salt and freshly
ground black pepper, to taste

*The success of this soup lies in its foundations. They must be strong,
resilient, and yet also concealed. In Italian cuisine, these foundations
are often a* battuto — *carrot, celery and onion — gently fried in oil, to
which legumes, grains (or pasta) and vegetables are added.*

*Mum's minestrone (a regular at our dinner table) followed a loose
recipe that was versatile and yet anchored to a recurrent set of flavours:
the* battuto, *some borlotti beans and a handful of pearl barley. The rest
changed according to her whim, what we had on hand, and the seasons.
This is the autumn/winter version. In spring, peas, asparagus and broad
beans replace pumpkin and potato (see* Minestrone Primavera *on page
172). In summer, when courgettes and tomatoes are in full swing, they
work their way in.*

Drain the beans and rinse them well. Transfer to a large pan, and cover
with double the volume of cold water. Place over a medium heat and
bring to the boil. Cook for about 40 minutes from when the water starts
to boil, or until tender but still holding their shape. Save about 250 ml |
1 cup of the cooking water, then drain the beans and set aside.

Heat the oil in a large, heavy-based pan. Add the onion, carrots and
celery (the *battuto*) and fry gently until tender, about 8 minutes, stirring
occasionally. Next, add the pumpkin, potato and barley. Pour in the
bean cooking liquid plus enough cold water to cover; throw in the
chunks of Parmesan rind. Cover with a lid and cook for 25–30 minutes,
or until the vegetables are tender and the pumpkin has tinted the broth
with a warm orange hue.

Now add the beans, taste and season accordingly. Carry on cooking for
10 more minutes, then remove the soup from the heat and allow it to
cool slightly, about 10 minutes. Serve with the chopped parsley, black
pepper and a drizzle of olive oil. And if you don't want to eat it right
away, it'll be even more flavoursome after a night's rest.

Bean & Pasta Soup

SERVES 4

- 400g | 14oz dried borlotti beans, soaked overnight
- 50g | 1¾oz piece of salt-cured lardo
- Small bunch of flat-leaf parsley, leaves picked
- 1 golden onion, thinly sliced
- 30ml | 2 tablespoons extra virgin olive oil
- 1 litre | 4¼ cups vegetable stock, heated
- 100g | 3½oz ditalini or tubetti pasta (or other short round pasta)
- Fine-grain sea salt and freshly ground black pepper, to taste
- Grana Padano, grated, to serve (optional)

In compiling the list of recipes for this book, I soon realised that some dishes in this section would be a collection of Great-Grandma Maria's favourites: her culinary legacy survives her.

Maria, Mum's grandmother, was the official cook in the family. She loved cooking above everything, particularly dusting and ironing and doing the laundry. She claimed she was too old for such chores, so she made a deal with Grandma and offered to take care of the cooking in exchange for not having to deal with housework. Grandma agreed; the whole family seemed relieved at the idea of having more of Maria's food on their table.

During the week, when the meals mostly consisted of menestra de fasoi *(bean soup and pasta) and polenta, Maria could be heard making a base for the soup in the wee hours of the morning. Old knife in one hand — perhaps sharpened once in a blue moon by the* arrotino *— and an even older wooden board in the other, she would go* tac tac tac . . . *until a pile of onions, parsley and slices of salt-cured* lardo *had all given way to a creamy, bright-green paste, which was then fried in oil and destined to flavour a good deal of beans.*

A soup made of pasta and beans was something people ate on a daily basis in the area: it was nourishing, cheap and filling, if a bit repetitive. We don't eat menestra de fasoi *every day anymore, just often enough to be reminded of how much we like it, especially on a winter day, hands wrapped around the bowl, and a wonderful scent of nutty beans and fresh parsley coming up in steamy swirls, warming the body from the inside out.*

CONTINUED OVERLEAF

Note: Like most soups in this book, this *menestra* can be made ahead and warmed up when required. In fact, it might as well benefit from a night's rest, for the resting time gives its flavours the chance to expand and deepen. Just add more hot vegetable stock when you reheat it to bring its texture back to 'soupy'.

Drain the beans and rinse them well. Transfer to a large pan, and cover with double the volume of cold water. Place over a medium heat and bring to the boil. Cook for about 40 minutes from when the water starts to boil, or until tender but still holding their shape. Save about 250 ml | 1 cup of the cooking water, then drain the beans and set aside.

Using a sharp knife, mince the *lardo* into a somewhat creamy mixture. Chop the parsley leaves very finely and then start mincing this and the onion together with the *lardo*, until you obtain a sort of green paste. This is your *battuto*.

Heat the olive oil in a large, heavy-based pan. Add the *battuto* and fry until the onion is soft and translucent. At this point, stir in about two-thirds of the beans and move them around to coat them in fat. Fry for about 5 minutes, stirring often, and then cover with the hot stock and the reserved bean liquid. Reduce the heat and simmer, covered, for about 15 minutes, until the beans are very tender and almost falling apart. Remove from the heat and blend (I now use a hand-held stick blender; in the past they used a food mill) until smooth, then taste and season accordingly.

Place the broth back over a medium heat. When the liquid starts to boil again, add the rest of the beans and the pasta. Cook for 10 minutes, or until the pasta is tender but al dente, stirring frequently. Remove from the heat and allow the soup to rest for 15 minutes. Serve with a generous dusting of grated Grana Padano, if you like.

RISOTTO DE BRUSCANDOLI
Wild Hop Risotto

SERVES 4

300g | 10½oz young wild
    hop shoots, bottom ends
    trimmed

75g | ⅓ cup unsalted butter

½ golden onion, finely
    chopped

360g | heaped 1¾ cups
    risotto rice (Vialone Nano
    or Carnaroli)

120ml | ½ cup dry white wine

1.5 litres | 6¼ cups vegetable
    stock, heated

50g | 1¾oz Grana Padano,
    grated

Fine-grain sea salt and freshly
    ground black pepper, to taste

I learnt to forage at an early age. Uncle Renato taught me — what to look for and where — at a time when my main interests ranged from hide-and-seek to skipping rope. Come to think of it, he taught me a good deal of things: he had me listen to Led Zeppelin, The Beatles, David Bowie and the best Italian songwriters on his record player; he taught me card tricks; he mentored me in tennis; and yes, he trained me in weed picking, and managed to make it seem very cool at the same time.

Many times we delved into pine forests to pick wild asparagus, crossed untouched fields looking for poppy leaves, and strolled along riverbanks in search of bruscandoli *(wild hop shoots). The scene of our first* bruscandoli *hunt is engrained in my memory. We were out for a walk along the river one day when he spotted a few shoots poking from the side of the road. In a matter of seconds, he disappeared down the slope and re-emerged with a bunch of bouncy green curls, a spark of triumph in his eyes.*

As soon as we reached home, without saying one word, he handed our foraging bounty to Grandma, who knew exactly what to do. She headed to the kitchen and came back half an hour later with a steaming pot of risotto, flecked with maroon bruscandoli. *I was starving and pretty much inhaled the whole thing, but couldn't help noticing that it had a peculiar flavour to it — musky, a bit resinous and definitely 'wild'.*

In Veneto, bruscandoli *are intrinsically bound to many iconic springtime dishes. Flavour-wise, they are akin to wild asparagus, but retain a distinctive aromatic character that is reminiscent of pale ale and young rosemary. Many food writers sang their praises. Elizabeth David, for one, devoted a beautiful essay to their unique flavour and fleeting nature. And fleeting they are indeed: at the market, they disappear in the blink of an eye; while in the fields they turn woody at the first spring heatwave.*

However briefly they may last, risotto remains Venetians' favourite way to enjoy them. And it is a risotto without many embellishments, for the spark these tiny shoots give off is quite impressive. Which is why, in its essence, this recipe can be read as a paradigm; it's good for many other shoots and leaves, such as wild asparagus, nettles — just about anything that grows in your backyard in the spring and is good enough to eat.

Note: Whenever I make risotto, I use a wooden spoon with a hole. It's perfect for letting the rice flow through without crushing it, and at the same time, it helps trap more air bubbles in the mixture, producing a creamier, lighter risotto.

Bring a medium pan of water to the boil. Blanch the shoots for 2–3 minutes, drain and transfer to an ice bath to keep them snappy and bright green. Once cooled, chop them roughly and set aside.

In a wide, heavy-based pan, melt a large knob of the butter, about 30g | 2 tablespoons. When hot and bubbly, add the chopped onion and fry gently until soft and translucent, stirring often so it doesn't colour. Next, add the rice; toast it for a couple of minutes, stirring often, until it turns opaque and you hear it hissing. Pour in the wine: it should whoosh as it hits the pan; increase the heat if not. Allow it to evaporate and then stir in the *bruscandoli* and a first splash of stock.

Cook the risotto by adding the hot stock a little at the time, allowing the rice to absorb most of the liquid before adding some more. Carry on this way until the rice feels tender but still al dente, around 15 minutes. Taste and season a couple of times throughout this process, and then once more at the end.

When ready, remove the risotto from the heat, cover with a lid and leave to rest for a couple of minutes. Uncover, add a generous splash of stock (aim for a loose texture), the remaining butter and the grated Grana and whip everything energetically until fully incorporated. Serve immediately.

Rice & Pea Soup

SERVES 4

1kg | 2lb 3oz unshelled
  fresh peas

1.5 litres | 6¼ cups chicken
  or vegetable stock, heated

30g | 1oz piece of flat pancetta

2 tablespoons finely chopped
  flat-leaf parsley leaves

½ golden onion, finely
  chopped

15ml | 1 tablespoon
  extra virgin olive oil

15g | 1 tablespoon unsalted
  butter

300g | 1½ cups risotto rice
  (Vialone Nano or Carnaroli)

50g | 1¾oz Grana Padano,
  grated

Fine-grain sea salt and freshly
  ground black pepper, to taste

Note: Don't be shy with the
peas — the more the merrier.
As a rule of thumb, use 3 parts
unshelled peas to 1 part rice.

An iconic Venetian dish, risi e bisi is a dense soup of rice and peas within a pea-flavoured broth. Traditionally, it is linked to the festivity of Saint Mark's Day, patron saint of Venice, on twenty-fifth April. Venetians would crowd around the stalls of the Rialto Market to secure their share of fresh peas, the first of the season, arriving from the vegetable gardens of the island of Sant'Erasmo, then rush home to join in the culinary celebrations. The tradition slowly spread from the floating city to the inland and eventually reached every corner of the region, elevating risi e bisi *to the status of iconic dish.*

Shell the peas, reserving the pods. Place the peas in a small pan with 30ml | 2 tablespoons of the stock and simmer over a low heat until bright green and al dente. Remove from the heat and set aside. Wash the pods and place them in a large pan together with the rest of the stock. Bring everything to a simmer and cook over a low heat for about 20 minutes. Keep warm.

Cut the pancetta very finely — almost to a mince. Incorporate the chopped parsley and onion and carry on mincing until you have a fine, even mixture. This is your *battuto*.

Heat the oil and butter in a heavy-based pan over a medium heat. Add the *battuto* mix and fry gently until the onion looks soft and translucent. Add the rice and toast it for a couple of minutes, stirring often, then cover with the strained hot pea stock.

Cook the rice for about 10 minutes, stirring often so that it doesn't stick to the bottom. At this point, add the reserved peas and season with salt and pepper. Carry on cooking for 5 more minutes, or until the rice is tender and has absorbed most of the liquid. If the soup is too dense add a few spoonfuls of hot water to loosen it up (it should be looser than a risotto). Finish with a generous dusting of grated Grana Padano.

Rice & Pumpkin Soup

SERVES 4

30g | 2 tablespoons unsalted
  butter
1 golden onion, finely chopped
800g | 1lb 12oz pumpkin,
  peeled and cut into 3cm |
  1.2 inch chunks
1.5 litres | 6¼ cups vegetable
  or chicken stock, heated
250g | 1¼ cups risotto rice
  (such as Vialone Nano
  or Carnaroli)
100g | 3½oz Italian pork
  sausage, crumbled (optional)
50g | 1¾oz Grana Padano,
  grated
Fine-grain sea salt and freshly
  ground black pepper, to taste

Note: Like *risi e bisi* (see
page 53), this is considered a
menestra (soup) rather than
a risotto; the difference being
not so much in the density as
in the way the rice is cooked.

There's a lot to love about this thrifty Venetian soup, not least the fact that it provides warmth and comfort with little to no effort. Funnily enough, it never ranked in Mum's list of favourites — she found certain kinds of pumpkin 'sickeningly sweet' — though she would happily make it for us whenever Grandma gifted us with one of her home-grown pumpkins.

Mum's trick to balance the sweet inclinations of this soup is to enhance its savoury side by means of some crumbled fresh salame or sausage. The fact that this addition wasn't very traditional didn't bother her (who complains about sausage?). Ultimately, though, it all boils down to personal taste. Leave the sausage out and you'll have one of the oldest Venetian soups out there.

In a wide, heavy-based pan, melt the butter and, when hot and bubbly, add the chopped onion and fry gently until soft and translucent, stirring often so it doesn't colour. Stir in the pumpkin and cook over a medium-low heat until just softened on the outside, stirring frequently. Pour in the hot stock and cover. Reduce the heat and simmer until the pumpkin falls apart. Remove from the heat and blend until smooth. Taste and season with salt and pepper.

Place the pan of pumpkin stock back over a medium heat and, as soon as it comes back to the boil, add the rice. Cook for about 15 minutes, or until the rice feels tender and the soup has turned dense and creamy; stir often to prevent the rice from sticking to the bottom. Remove from the heat and allow it to cool slightly.

Meanwhile, if using, fry the crumbled sausage in a dry frying pan until browned and cooked through. Stir it into the soup at the very last minute alongside the grated Grana. Serve with a generous dose of freshly ground black pepper.

Chicken Liver Risotto

SERVES 4

75g | ⅓ cup unsalted butter

30ml | 2 tablespoons extra
  virgin olive oil

½ golden onion, finely
  chopped

450g | 1lb chicken livers,
  roughly chopped

15ml | 1 tablespoon white
  wine vinegar

180ml | ¾ cup dry white wine

30g | 2 tablespoons
  tomato purée (optional)

Pinch of ground cinnamon

360g | heaped 1¾ cups
  risotto rice (Vialone Nano
  or Carnaroli)

1.5 litres | 6¼ cups chicken
  stock, heated

50g | 1¾oz Grana Padano,
  grated

Fine-grain sea salt and freshly
  ground black pepper, to taste

This risotto is one of Grandma's specialities, of the kind she'd prepare when we were invited for Sunday lunch, particularly on the occasions of the sagra paesana, *the village fair occurring in early October. Her insistence on this dish was purely ritualistic, honouring a long-held Venetian tradition whereby a soup of chicken liver and rice (called* minestra della festa*) was served at weddings and family celebrations.*

Grandma's risotto — a slight evolution of said minestra della festa *— didn't include just chicken livers, but the rest of the edible entrails too: heart, gizzards and bits of stomach for good measure.*

For this book, I have changed the recipe a fair bit, mostly to make it more accessible and a tad easier on the palate. The main difference resides in the sole inclusion of chicken livers, which are easy to come across and are often appreciated by a wide crowd; and in the addition of the ever-useful acidity of vinegar — the secret ingredient of Venetian cuisine — to mitigate the metallic notes of the liver. Cinnamon, for its part, comes into play to give warmth and a patina of renaissance to an otherwise timeless dish.

Heat a small knob of the butter (about 15g | 1 tablespoon) and the olive oil in a medium frying pan. When sizzling, add half of the onion and fry gently until soft and translucent. Stir in the chicken livers and allow to brown, stirring frequently, for about 5 minutes. At this point, pour in the vinegar and one-third of the wine and let them evaporate, stirring often. Add the tomato purée, if using, and allow it to dissolve in the liquid and coat the livers. Moments before turning off the heat, add the cinnamon and season with salt and a generous dose of black pepper.

Melt another large knob of butter (about 30g | 2 tablespoons) in a wide, heavy-based pan. When hot and bubbly, add the remaining chopped onion and fry gently until soft and translucent, stirring often so it doesn't colour. Next, add the rice; toast it for a couple of minutes, stirring often, until it turns opaque and you hear it hissing. Pour in the remaining wine: it should whoosh as it hits the pan; increase the heat if not. Allow it to evaporate and then stir in the cooked chicken livers and a first splash of stock.

Cook the risotto by adding hot stock a little at the time, allowing the rice to absorb most of the liquid before adding some more. Carry on this way until the rice feels tender but still al dente, around 15 minutes. Taste and season a couple of times throughout this process, and then once more at the end.

When ready, remove the risotto from the heat, cover with a lid and leave to rest for a couple of minutes. Uncover, add a generous splash of stock (aim for a loose texture), the remaining butter and the grated Grana Padano and whip everything energetically until fully incorporated. Serve immediately.

Tagliatelle with Rabbit Ragù

SERVES 4

For the rabbit ragù:

45g | 3 tablespoons unsalted butter

30ml | 2 tablespoons extra virgin olive oil

100g | 3½oz piece of flat pancetta, minced

1 golden onion, finely chopped

1 small carrot, peeled and finely diced

1 celery stick, trimmed and finely chopped

3 sage leaves

1 sprig of rosemary

1 medium farmyard or wild rabbit, cleaned and boned (yielding about 500g | 1lb 2oz meat), meat finely chopped

180ml | ¾ cup dry white wine

480ml | 2 cups vegetable stock, heated, or as needed

45ml | 3 tablespoons tomato sauce (passata)

15g | 1 tablespoon tomato purée

Fine-grain sea salt and freshly ground black pepper, to taste

To serve:

450g | 1lb fresh egg tagliatelle (see Notes overleaf if you want to make your own)

100g | 3½oz Grana Padano, grated

If I could eat tagliatelle with rabbit ragù every week, I would. I don't, but Mum used to, for Great-Grandma Maria was adamant about making it every Sunday as the first course, followed, most likely, by braised rabbit (see page 74) and stir-fried greens (see pages 90 and 209). Then again, they did rear their own rabbits.

Rabbits have been farmed for centuries in Veneto, and the tradition continues to this day, with rabbit being widely available in butcher shops and on restaurant menus. Many agriturismi *dotting the Venetian countryside serve it, either on its own or, if you're lucky, as part of an always delightful* ragù di cortile *(a 'courtyard' mixed-meat ragù).*

Great-Grandma Maria only used rabbit in her ragù. The sauce started with rabbit meat browning in a glistening puddle of butter and pancetta. It was then wetted by wine and broth and a blushing bit of tomato before being simmered patiently for a good while — long enough for Maria to make a batch of fresh tagliatelle to go with it.

Making fresh pasta was part of the Sunday ritual in rural Veneto. No woman would ever get married, let alone be allowed in the kitchen, if she didn't know how to tame a ball of dough. Maria used to stretch her dough with a rolling pin (baco da taiadele), cut the tagliatelle by hand, and hang them to dry around the kitchen like frilly fringes. No pasta machine in her kitchen.

I wish I could say the same. These days, I not only rely on a pasta machine, but I often depend on a good fresh pasta supplier, too. The rabbit sauce, however, has no shortcuts: its therapeutic properties rest in the cooking as much as in the eating. Taking a half Sunday to bring it all together seems like a luxury sometimes, but it all feels very worthwhile the moment we sit down to lunch.

CONTINUED OVERLEAF

Notes: Make fresh pasta by working together 300g | 2 cups plain '00' flour with 3 eggs. Wrap the dough in cling film and rest for 1 hour, then roll very thinly using a pasta machine. Finally cut into 5mm- | ¼-inch thick strips and hang to dry for 1 hour prior to cooking.

This ragù goes well with a wide range of pastas. In Veneto, aside from tagliatelle, you often see it served with fresh *bigoli*, but quality durum wheat *maccheroni rigati* are also great here. As for the rabbit, opt for a farmyard kind from a trusted source, or else a wild rabbit: the two will differ in flavour but will both taste good (unlike intensively raised rabbit, which is tasteless). If you have the chance, ask your butcher to bone your rabbit, as it's a fairly tedious process.

Heat the butter and oil in a large heavy-based pan set over a medium heat. Once hot, add the pancetta and pan-fry it until browned and crisp, about 2 minutes. Next, add the onion, carrot, celery, sage and rosemary and cook until the vegetables are very tender, 4–5 minutes, stirring often. At this point, stir in the chopped rabbit meat and increase the heat to medium-high. Brown it on all sides for about 5 minutes, then pour in the wine, stock, tomato sauce and tomato purée. Once the sauce is simmering again, reduce the heat and cover.

Cook the ragù for about 1 hour, stirring occasionally and adding more stock if the liquid reduces too quickly. By the end you should have a red-blushed, thick sauce with meat that almost falls apart. Taste and adjust the seasoning; discard the sage and rosemary, remove from the heat, and set aside.

Next, bring a large pan of salted water to a rolling boil. Lower in the tagliatelle and cook for 3–4 minutes, (the exact time depends on the type of pasta). Meanwhile, set the rabbit ragù back over a medium heat. When the pasta is ready, drain it and top it with the ragù. Toss until any water has been absorbed and the pasta is well coated in the sauce.

Serve with a generous dusting of Grana.

Bigoli with Duck Ragù

SERVES 4

For the duck ragù:

30ml | 2 tablespoons extra
  virgin olive oil

2 garlic cloves, whole but
  lightly crushed

2 sprigs of rosemary

500g | 1lb 2oz minced duck
  meat (ideally from Barbary
  or Muscovy duck), including
  fat and skin

240ml | 1 cup dry white wine

480ml | 2 cups duck stock
  (see Note overleaf) or
  vegetable stock, or as
  needed, heated

2 juniper berries

Fine-grain sea salt and freshly
  ground black pepper, to taste

To serve:

500g | 1lb 2oz fresh *bigoli*
  (or use thick fresh spaghetti)

100g | 3½oz Grana Padano,
  grated

The diversity of landscapes and climates in the various corners of Veneto has a direct impact on its gastronomic wealth. On one side you have the lagoon and the sea, on the other the temperate shores of Lake Garda. In the north, picturesque hills precede the imposing advance of the Alpine peaks; while in the south, rivers, canals and Italy's largest delta form an intricate pattern over the fertile flatlands. It is perhaps this last aspect that has had the biggest impact on the food that is consumed in the corner of Venetian inland in which I grew up — the abundance of water.

Take duck, for example. Ducks proliferate and thrive where there's water, which is why they have been successfully reared in the area for centuries, becoming the main feature of many iconic 'land' (as opposed to 'sea') dishes. Alongside the wild specimens that populate the Venetian lagoon and the wetlands of the Po Delta, there are those that are raised on farms: breeds of all kinds, raised extensively and destined for the highest culinary purposes.

Among them, the most valued (due to its tender, flavoursome red meat and lower fat content) is the anitra muta *(anara muta in dialect), i.e. the Barbary or Muscovy duck. In the past, one would still be able to find it in the wild, but farmyard-bred birds are just as delicious, if raised well and left free to roam (and swim!) and feed on grass as much as cereal. And they make perfect ragù for a steamy bowl of bigoli.*

Bigoli (bigoi *in dialect) is long pasta that is typical of Veneto. Depending on the area, they can be fresh or dry, wholemeal or white. People who owned a* bigolaro *(the specific pasta press used to extrude* bigoli*) used to make them at home; those living in the city would have had access to fresh* bigoli *from the deli. The rest had to make do with the dry version.*

Bigoli con l'anara *(with duck ragù) is a speciality of Vicenza and Padua. In Venice and thereabouts, one would be more likely to see this ragù spooned over a bowl of potato gnocchi or gnocchetti (see page 174). Both are delightful but, for once, I betray my province of origin and favour Vicenza's version, mostly because I have eaten it so many times over day trips across the region and around the Colli Berici that it has become part of my culinary education.*

Note: To make duck stock, ask your butcher for some duck bones, ideally with a little meat still attached. Place the bones in a pan with a peeled carrot, 2 celery sticks, a quartered onion, a small bunch of parsley and 3 litres | 12½ cups of water. Bring everything to the boil and simmer very slowly for about 2 hours, skimming frequently. Once done, strain the broth and use as in the recipe.

Heat the oil in a large, heavy-based pan set over a medium heat. Once hot, add the garlic and rosemary and allow them to infuse the oil for a couple of minutes, stirring often. Next, add the duck mince and increase the heat to medium-high. Cook for 4–5 minutes, until evenly browned; season generously. Pour in the wine and stock and add the juniper berries. Bring everything to a simmer and then reduce the heat to the minimum and cover with a lid.

Cook the ragù for at least 1 hour, stirring occasionally and adding a little stock if the ragù becomes too dry. Once the liquid has reduced completely and only an oily sauce remains, remove from the heat and discard the rosemary, juniper and garlic. Cover and keep warm.

Finally, bring a large pan of salted water to a rolling boil. Lower in the *bigoli* and cook them for 5–6 minutes if fresh, about 10 minutes if dry (the exact time will depend on the type of pasta; try to keep it al dente). Meanwhile, set the ragù back over a medium heat. When the pasta is ready, drain and top it with the meat sauce and half of the grated Grana Padano. Toss until any water has been absorbed and the pasta is evenly seasoned.

Serve the *bigoli* alongside the rest of the grated cheese.

Bigoli with Anchovies & Onions

SERVES 4

100g | 3½oz oil-packed
  anchovy fillets, drained
  (or 8 large salted sardines)
80ml | ⅓ cup extra virgin
  olive oil
2 golden onions (about
  400g | 14oz), thinly sliced
80ml | ⅓ cup hot water
400g | 14oz dry wholemeal
  bigoli (or use thick spaghetti
  or 500g | 1lb 2oz fresh
  bigoli — see Notes below)
Pinch of ground cinnamon
  (optional)
Fine-grain sea salt and freshly
  ground black pepper, to taste

Notes: If you can't get *bigoli*,
opt for thick bronze-die
vermicelli or another form
of thick spaghetti.

I included both the traditional
version with sardines and the
revised one with anchovies.
Choose according to your
taste and bravery.

A dish of Jewish origin, bigoi in salsa *has become a classic Venetian pasta dish that is typically consumed on fasting (meatless) days, though you'll now be able to find it on the menu of most* osterie *any time of the year.*

The version of bigoi in salsa *made with salted sardines is perhaps the most orthodox, but I personally find it a bit too sharp, preferring a more accessible, less imperious version with oil-packed anchovies.*

———

If using sardines, wash them thoroughly under cold running water to get rid of the salt. Pat dry and de-bone. Set aside.

Heat the oil in a large frying pan over low heat. Add the sliced onions and fry gently until very soft and translucent, about 10 minutes, stirring frequently to prevent them from browning. Pour over the hot water and carry on cooking and stirring the onions over a low heat until they have fallen apart, about 30 minutes.

Next, add the anchovy fillets (or sardines) and dissolve them into the onion sauce using the tip of a wooden spoon. Cook for 5–8 more minutes, until the sauce looks very creamy — the onions and anchovies should be mingled in a brownish, oily mixture. Remove from the heat and cover to keep warm.

Bring a large pan of water to a rolling boil. Salt the water and as soon as it starts boiling again, add the *bigoli*. Cook the pasta until just al dente, reserving a glass of cooking water for the sauce. Drain and transfer to the pan with the sauce and set over a medium-high heat. Toss, adding splashes of cooking water to help the sauce come together and coat the pasta. Finish with a couple of turns of the pepper grinder and a pinch of cinnamon, if you like. Toss once more and then serve.

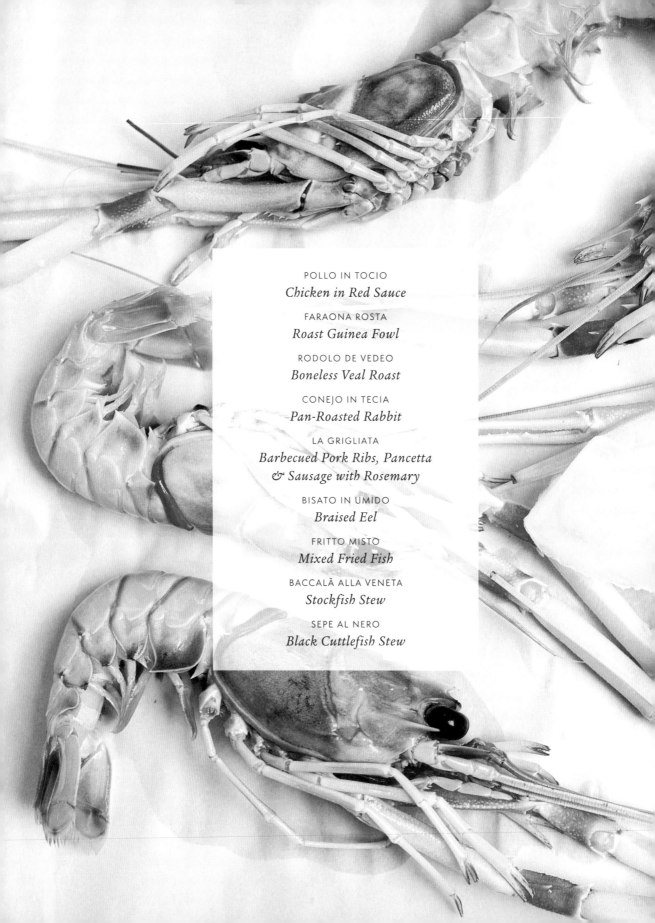

POLLO IN TOCIO
Chicken in Red Sauce

FARAONA ROSTA
Roast Guinea Fowl

RODOLO DE VEDEO
Boneless Veal Roast

CONEJO IN TECIA
Pan-Roasted Rabbit

LA GRIGLIATA
*Barbecued Pork Ribs, Pancetta
& Sausage with Rosemary*

BISATO IN UMIDO
Braised Eel

FRITTO MISTO
Mixed Fried Fish

BACCALÀ ALLA VENETA
Stockfish Stew

SEPE AL NERO
Black Cuttlefish Stew

SECONDI

POLLO IN TOCIO
Chicken in Red Sauce

SERVES 4

30ml | 2 tablespoons
  extra virgin olive oil

30g | 2 tablespoons
  unsalted butter

1 free-range chicken (about
  1.5kg | 3lb 5oz), cut into
  6–8 pieces (see Note below)

½ golden onion, finely
  chopped

½ carrot, peeled and
  finely diced

½ celery stick, trimmed and
  finely chopped

2 garlic cloves, whole but
  lightly crushed

120ml | ½ cup dry white wine

30g | 2 tablespoons
  tomato purée

Fine-grain sea salt and freshly
  ground black pepper, to taste

Note: To recreate the flavour
of the old days, a free-range
(*ruspante*), preferably organic
bird would be best, as it'll not
only have better flavour and
texture, but it'll also stand
up to slow-braising without
falling apart and releasing
excess liquid.

Great-Grandma Maria was not shy about picking up a bird from the family chicken coop, dispatching it, plucking it and pan roasting it for the family dinner. Her chicken drenched in tomato sauce — slow-cooked on the wood-fire stove and vaguely smoky — remains one of dishes for which she's most remembered, and missed.

———————

Heat the oil and butter in a heavy-based braising pan large enough to fit the chicken pieces in a single layer. Once hot and bubbly, add the chicken, skin-side down, and cook until it has turned golden brown, about 7–8 minutes. Turn the pieces and brown them on the other side for about the same amount of time. Transfer them to a plate and set aside for a moment.

In the same pan, add the *battuto* (onion, carrot and celery) and the garlic. Cook the vegetables until soft, about 5 minutes, and then return the chicken to the pan. Turn the heat to medium-high and add the wine. Leave it to evaporate until reduced by half, then add the tomato purée whisked together with 60ml water. Stir to coat the chicken in the sauce. Season generously, reduce the heat to low and cover with a lid.

Cook the chicken for 40–45 minutes or until tender and done all the way through. During this time, check that the liquid doesn't reduce excessively — add a splash of water to keep things 'saucy' if necessary. Once done, remove from the heat and allow it to rest for 10 minutes before serving.

FARAONA ROSTA
Roast Guinea Fowl

SERVES 6

1 medium free-range guinea
    fowl (about 1.2kg | 2lb 10oz),
    plucked, gutted, head and
    feet removed
2 sprigs of rosemary
5–6 sage leaves
4 garlic cloves, whole but
    lightly crushed
30g | 2 tablespoons unsalted
    butter, softened
180ml | ¾ cup chicken or
    vegetable stock, heated
Fine-grain sea salt and freshly
    ground black pepper

Note: In parts of Veneto, a
sauce called *pearà* or *peverada*
is traditionally served with
faraona. The sauce, made
with chicken and fowl livers,
salame, anchovies, capers,
parsley and loads of black
pepper, has ancient origins,
and is especially used in the
area around Verona. In my
family it wasn't customary,
so I didn't include it here.
If the sound of it fascinates
you, feel free to give it a try;
recipes for it are easy to find.

In the realm of traditional Venetian secondi, *roast guinea fowl scores pretty high in popularity. It certainly scores high in Grandma's mind. The day I told her I was moving to London she tried to convince me to take a guinea fowl in my suitcase. Frozen, of course, but still! She must have thought that it would make me feel more 'at home', a way to mitigate the initial nostalgia by means of a homely Sunday meal.*

Guinea fowl is darker than chicken, but less so than pheasant. If you like the full flavour of dark meat but don't appreciate it being gamey, guinea fowl is a good option. This is especially true for farmed fowl that has been allowed to roam freely, perhaps even fly around a bit, and that has been raised without rushing: it's exponentially tastier than one that has had a brief and intense life.

Even though it tends to be larger in size, guinea fowl can be cooked in the same ways chicken can. Roasted might seem banal, but it's always a winner, not least because it needs little tending, and is always deeply comforting.

———

Preheat the oven to 200°C | 390°F | gas mark 6. Using a lighter, singe the skin of the guinea fowl to get rid of any residual plumage. Stuff it with the rosemary, sage and garlic, smear it all over with the butter and season generously with salt and pepper.

Place the bird in a buttered roasting tin and cover with foil. Set on the middle rack of the oven and roast for about 40 minutes. Next, add the stock and roast, uncovered, for a further 40 minutes, until the bird is cooked through and browned all over (check that the inner temperature has reached 75°C | 170°F, using a probe thermometer, or else check that the juices run clear when pierced between leg and thigh). Serve as you would a classic roast, with your preferred accompaniments.

Boneless Veal Roast

SERVES 6

1.2–1.5kg | 2lb 10oz–3lb 5oz rolled loin or shoulder roast of veal (ask your butcher to bone, roll and tie the meat for you)

100g | 3½oz thinly sliced flat pancetta

45g | 3 tablespoons unsalted butter

5 garlic cloves, whole but lightly crushed

2 sprigs of rosemary

120ml | ½ cup dry white wine

420ml | 1¾ cup vegetable stock, heated

Fine-grain sea salt and freshly ground black pepper, to taste

Grandma's Sunday meal wasn't complete without a slice of veal roast. Sure, we had already gone through a course of mushroom risotto, followed by roasted guinea fowl, mashed potatoes and stir-fried greens (see pages 72, 101, 90 and 209); but who was going to say no to a slice of veal with a second round of mash?

Veal is controversial. Not quite like horse, or donkey — both of which are considered perfectly fine to eat in Veneto, as in many other Italian regions — but somewhere along that path. When I eat it, I make sure that the meat comes from an animal that has had a decent, albeit short, life. If you enjoy veal on occasion, this no-frills, lovely roast is a good place to start, and a way to let the flavour of the meat shine through.

———————

Preheat the oven to 160°C | 320°F | gas mark 3. Line one side of the veal loin with pancetta and season with salt and pepper. Tie it tightly with cooking twine (again, you can ask your butcher to this for you).

Heat the butter in a heavy-based roasting pan or a deep, flameproof casserole dish, large enough to accommodate the meat. When bubbly, stir in the garlic and the rosemary. Let these infuse the butter for half a minute and then remove the aromatics and add the meat. Sear it for about 10–15 minutes, until browned all over. Next, pour in the wine and stock, return the aromatics, cover with foil and transfer to the oven.

Roast for about 1½ hours, or until the inner temperature has reached 70°C | 160°F (the exact cooking time will depend on the actual weight of the meat; calculate about 40 minutes for every 500g | 1lb 2oz); baste the meat frequently during the entire cooking. At the very end, turn on the grill and allow the pancetta to crisp up for about 5 minutes. Remove from the oven and rest for 20 minutes, then untie and slice. Keep the meat warm.

Strain any remaining cooking juices (discard the garlic and rosemary) and place in a small pan. Bring to the boil and simmer until the sauce has reduced to about one-third of its initial volume. Taste and add salt if needed. Serve with the sliced veal.

Pan-Roasted Rabbit

SERVES 4–6

30ml | 2 tablespoons extra
  virgin olive oil
30g | 2 tablespoons
  unsalted butter
90g | 3oz piece of smoked
  pancetta, minced
2 garlic cloves, whole but
  lightly crushed
2 sprigs of rosemary
1 whole farmyard or wild
  rabbit (about 1kg | 2lb 3oz),
  cut into 8 pieces
120ml | ½ cup dry white wine
240ml | 1 cup vegetable stock,
  heated, or as needed
Fine-grain sea salt and freshly
  ground black pepper, to taste

Note: Rabbit, particularly
if wild, can be soaked
overnight in acidulated water
(following the ratio of 15ml
| 1 tablespoon of white wine
vinegar per litre | 4¼ cups
of water) to lessen the 'wild'
flavour. The pieces of rabbit
should be completely covered
in liquid and stored in the
fridge, then rinsed thoroughly
and patted dry before
proceeding with the recipe.
Alternatively, if rabbit is not
your thing, farmyard chicken
makes a fine substitute.

One from Great-Grandma Maria's repertoire: a slow-braised rabbit for il pranzo della domenica (Sunday lunch). This is a recipe in bianco, meaning 'in white' or without sauce. White it is not, however, for the gravy is anything but clear. In fact, as the meat cooks, the essences mingle with the bronzed juices of pancetta, butter and oil. Maria liked to use all three of them, especially with rabbit, a notoriously lean meat, and I do the same, as each contributes to the complexity of the dish.

In tecia literally means 'in the pan' and describes the common Venetian practice of cooking rabbit on the stove. Maria, for her part, used to cook her rabbit on the wood-fire stove; a method, I am told, that imparted a strangely pleasant smokiness to the dish. A way to draw near this original flavour is to use smoked pancetta; speck is also nice, but less fatty. As for the type of tecia, a copper or cast-iron pan is best, though any sturdy braising pan will do just fine.

Heat the oil and butter in a heavy-based braising pan large enough to fit the meat in a single layer. Once hot and bubbly, add the pancetta and fry over a medium-high heat for a couple of minutes, until the fat has rendered. Next, stir in the garlic and rosemary and let them flavour the fat for 2–3 minutes, stirring occasionally. Add the pieces of rabbit and increase the heat. Brown on both sides, season, and then pour in the wine and allow it to evaporate. Finally, add the stock, reduce the heat to a gentle simmer, and cover with a lid.

Cook for 25 minutes, then turn the pieces and cook for a further 25 minutes. Check the pan regularly and add more wine or stock if needed — the rabbit should always be cooking in a little liquid. Once the time is up, uncover the pan, adjust the seasoning, and reduce the cooking juices for 5–7 minutes, or until only a thick, glistening gravy remains. Remove from the heat and serve the meat in its own gravy.

Barbecued Pork Ribs, Pancetta & Sausage with Rosemary

SERVES 4

20 sprigs of rosemary
4 Italian pork sausages
  (about 250g | 9oz each)
8 × 3mm- | 0.1-inch-thick
  slices of pork belly
  (fresh pancetta)
8 pork ribs

At the start of May, the village is alive with the smell of grilled meat. In addition to the first impromptu barbecues that the locals set up in their backyards, one must count the yearly food festival. For three weekends, the football field doubles up as a non-stop grilling hub, attracting meat-loving patrons from the whole province and capturing the local population in an irresistible smoky vortex.

The food offering has remained reassuringly unchanged: aside from the classic triplet of grilled pork belly, ribs and sausages, one can choose from a curated list of traditional primi piatti *and meat stews, though these hardly ever manage to steal the scene. In many years, I have never seen anyone not ordering the porky triad: they might have it preceded by a bowl of* bigoli, *and followed by a slice of crostata, but the triad is there, at the centre of the scene, where it should be.*

The barbecuing tradition is as strong in the village as it is in the whole of Veneto; in some areas, it coexists with another strong tradition — meat on a spit. Common grounds are the use of affordable pork cuts such as ribs and belly, and the outdoors-y, cheerful nature of it all. In this sense, the grigliata is a ritual that belongs to the warm season, with its long balmy nights and the sweet scent of sizzling sausages wafting in the wind.

Stick a sprig of rosemary into each of the pieces of meat (wet them before so they don't burn). You can then proceed 3 ways; I'll list them in order of personal preference.

METHOD 1: ON THE BARBECUE
The barbecue method depends on the kind of barbecue you have — gas, charcoal, with or without a lid, etc. In Italy, the most common sort is a charcoal (or even wood) barbecue with a metal wire set over the brazier, and no lid. Either way, get it fired as you normally would and then place the sausages, pork belly and ribs on the grill. Cook the meat on both sides, turning it often, until cooked through — the pork belly should be ready first, then the sausages, and then the ribs. The pork belly should be crisp on the edges and a bit curly, the meat browned. Always check

Note: A Venetian-style meat barbecue isn't complete without a side of grilled polenta (see page 36). Grill it in slices until nicely charred on both sides right after you finish with the meat. If you're cooking the meat in the oven, the polenta can be done in a griddle pan instead.

the ribs for doneness next to the bone. As for the sausages, you can cut them open (butterfly-style) to obtain a crisp inside. As soon as a piece of meat is done, transfer it to a large metal or aluminium platter and keep it warm. Serve as you go or as soon as you've finished.

METHOD 2: ON THE GRIDDLE

If you're not skilled with the barbecue, a cast-iron griddle delivers good results and it's a bit less messy — there's no fat falling on the charcoal and making a ton of smoke. Still, a good extractor fan in the kitchen or some form of ventilation helps. Heat the griddle over a medium-high heat for about 5 minutes — it must be very hot. Place the meat on top, in batches: start with the ribs, then the sausages, and finally the pork belly. Grill the meat on both sides, turning it often, until cooked through, checking for doneness as suggested in the method above. Transfer the cooked meat to a metal platter and keep it warm while you cook the rest. Eat as soon as you've finished.

METHOD 3: IN THE OVEN

The last-case scenario — good if you have bad ventilation in your house or don't want your hair to smell of campfire — is to bake the meat in the oven over a metal rack and with a tray set underneath to collect the drippings. Preheat the oven to 220°C | 430°F | gas mark 7, with said rack and tray set inside. As soon as the oven has come to temperature, remove the rack and tray from the oven and set the ribs and sausages on top. Bake for about 40 minutes, or until cooked through and crisp on the outside, turning them halfway through, and brushing them with their own fat if they appear too dry. After 20 minutes, add the pork belly. Cook for 10 minutes per side, or until crisp on the edges and nicely browned. Remove from the oven and serve.

BISATO IN UMIDO
Braised Eel

SERVES 4

2 eels (about 400g | 14oz
    each), cleaned (skinned,
    if you prefer) and cut into
    4 chunks each (ask your
    fishmonger to do it for you)
80ml | ⅓ cup white wine
    vinegar
30g | ¼ cup plain flour
30ml | 2 tablespoons extra
    virgin olive oil
2 garlic cloves, whole but
    lightly crushed
180ml | ¾ cup dry white wine
60g | ¼ cup tomato sauce
    (passata)
Fine-grain sea salt and freshly
    ground black pepper, to taste
1 tablespoon very finely
    chopped flat-leaf parsley
    leaves, to serve

One of the oldest Venetian recipes we have on record is called bisato su l'ara. *It consists of pieces of eel nestled among a host of bay leaves and cooked for hours in a clay pot on the cooling embers of the Murano glass furnaces.*

Eel used to abound in the rivers and lagoons of Veneto. Indeed when everything else failed and food was scarce (as happened often), locals knew that they could always go down to the water and catch a few water snakes. This abundance gave way to a wide array of recipes giving guidance on how to best enjoy this rich and nourishing creature. From chargrilled to braised, from deep-fried to roasted, the eel tradition flourished across the Venetian waterlands.

Things look very different these days. Eating habits have changed, of course, but also the fact that eel is now an endangered species means that it is only really consumed on special occasions. In Veneto, following a long-held custom of serving it on fasting days, eel is still traditionally eaten on Christmas Eve. Winter is a good time to enjoy it, for eel is in season, but also because the richness of the dish goes hand in hand with the indulgent spirit of the Christmas holidays.

In my family, eel used to be deep-fried or else braised in tomato sauce. The latter, in particular, makes for a saucy number that is heavy on the body but heavenly for the spirit. Removing the skin, though not compulsory, makes things lighter, while adding a splash of vinegar cuts through the unctuousness while also giving the sauce a pleasant sharpness that is quintessentially Venetian.

A lighter way to enjoy eel is chargrilled. Cut it into fillets (leave the skin on) and season with salt and pepper. Cover the embers with a good deal of ash so as to lower the heat (the fat released by the skin would otherwise provoke big flames), then grill on both sides until the skin has lost its oiliness and the flesh is cooked through (a fish griddle is helpful to avoid breaking the fillets when it's time to turn them).

VARIATION 2:

If you can't find eel, try mackerel. Get 8 mackerel fillets (skin on), roll them up and tie them with cooking twine. Follow the recipe, but reduce the braising time to 10 minutes.

Place the eels in a large bowl. Cover with cold water mixed with 60ml | ¼ cup of the vinegar and leave it to soak for 1 hour. Drain, rinse thoroughly and pat dry. Dust with flour and shake off any excess, then set aside.

Heat the oil with the garlic in a heavy-based pan. When hot, add the eel chunks and sear for 2 minutes each side, turning them with care so that they don't break up. Pour in the wine and allow it to evaporate, then add the tomato sauce diluted in 60ml | ¼ cup water. Reduce the heat, season with salt and pepper and cover with a lid.

Leave the eel to cook over a low heat for about 20 minutes, or until the flesh looks pearl-white and opaque and is cooked all the way through, adding a little water if the sauce starts to become too dry. Taste and adjust the seasoning, then pour in the rest of the vinegar, cover again and cook for a further 5 minutes, or until the sauce is thick and clings to the eel. Remove from the heat, top with parsley and serve.

Mixed Fried Fish

SERVES 4–6

200g | 7oz queen scallops
400g | 14oz raw prawns,
    shelled
300g | 10½oz fresh
    anchovies, gutted
300g | 10½oz small squid,
    cleaned, bodies cut into
    rings and tentacles cut
    into bite-sized pieces
150g | 1¼ cups plain
    flour, sifted
Sunflower oil, for frying
Fine-grain sea salt

Moreish is the first word that comes to mind when thinking of fritto misto. *Summer is the second. Salty, oily, crisp and utterly addictive, it's the quintessence of summertime in Veneto. No* ferragosto *(the Italian mid-summer holiday) goes by without us sitting under the pergola picking at a huge platter of mixed fried seafood, prosecco aplenty, and mosquitoes threatening our calves. It's traditional.*

The mix of fish in fritto misto *depends on a series of factors, most notably personal taste, seasonality and availability. In Venice, for example, squid rings, prawns and queen scallops are generally part of the medley alongside small-sized oily fish such as fresh anchovies and sardines.*

Regardless of what the ingredients list says, then, a good rule of thumb when making fritto misto *is to ask the fishmonger for advice on what's fresh, local and good for the frying pan; it always delivers the best results.*

Dust the fish in flour, shaking off any excess, and then transfer each type to a separate plate.

Fill two-thirds of a high-sided frying pan with sunflower oil. Place it over a medium-high heat, and wait until it reaches the right temperature (180°C | 350°F), which you can test with a thermometer or by inserting the handle of a wooden spoon in the oil; when small but fierce bubbles form around it, it's ready. (Alternatively, you can use a deep fryer, if you have one.)

Fry each type of fish in batches for 3–5 minutes, or until golden brown all over. Drain with a slotted spoon and transfer to a large platter covered with kitchen paper. Salt every batch and keep warm while you fry the next batch. Serve as soon as you finish, by itself or alongside a green salad.

BACCALÀ ALLA VENETA
Stockfish Stew

SERVES 6–8

1kg | 2lb 3oz stockfish
(ideally Ragno — see Note
on page 22)

300ml | 1¼ cups extra virgin
olive oil

2 golden onions, thinly sliced

5 oil-packed anchovy fillets,
drained

Leaves from a small bunch
of flat-leaf parsley, very
finely chopped

480ml | 2 cups whole milk

Fine-grain sea salt and freshly
ground black pepper, to taste

Baccalà is a dish that demands patience. It needs not to be tended, but to be awaited in its slow evolution from wood-like stockfish to creamy, melting, oily delight. The dry fish needs to be pounded vigorously and at length, then soaked for two days, and finally cooked for the good part of an afternoon — long enough for the flaky flesh to fall apart and for the house to be filled with its rich scent.

Unlike baccalà mantecato (see page 21), this recipe requires the fish to stew over a very low flame, so low that only one tiny bubble forms — a single, alchemic bubble. Throughout the long cooking process, the fish is repeatedly fed a mixture of oil and milk and an afterthought of anchovy, the flavour deepening at every addition, until it all comes together into a tempting ensemble of scents, tastes and textures.

On a large wooden board, pound the fish with a rolling pin (or a meat pounder). Cut it in pieces small enough to fit comfortably in your largest bowl. Cover with cold water and place in the fridge. Change the water twice a day for the following 48 hours.

When ready to make the *baccalà*, drain the cod and rinse well. Inspect the pieces and remove skin and bones. Rip the flesh into rough flakes and set aside.

Heat 30ml | 2 tablespoons of the oil in a large heavy-based pan set over a low heat. Add the onion and fry gently, until very soft and almost falling apart, stirring often. Next, stir in the anchovy fillets and allow them to dissolve. Add the stockfish, parsley, remaining oil and milk. Reduce the heat to low, cover and cook for 4½–5 hours (don't worry about overcooking it, as longer is usually better). Throughout this time, check it occasionally and add more milk and oil if it looks too dry — it should be creamy but not soupy. Towards the end, taste and season with salt and a generous dose of pepper.

Remove the *baccalà* from the heat and allow it rest for at least half an hour, or up to 1 day. Serve warm with grilled polenta.

SEPE AL NERO
Black Cuttlefish Stew

SERVES 4–6

1kg | 2lb 3oz cuttlefish, cleaned, ink sacs reserved (if your fishmonger cleans it for you, ask for the ink sacs; if you can't find cuttlefish with its ink, use bottled squid ink instead)

30ml | 2 tablespoons extra virgin olive oil

½ golden onion, finely chopped

120ml | ½ cup dry white wine

30ml | 2 tablespoons tomato sauce (passata)

300ml | 1¼ cups fish or vegetable stock, heated

Fine-grain sea salt and freshly ground black pepper, to taste

1 tablespoon very finely chopped flat-leaf parsley leaves, to serve

VARIATION:

Another classic Venetian dish is *seppie coi piselli* (cuttlefish with peas). The method is similar to that described here — simply skip the ink, double the tomato sauce and add roughly 300g | 10½oz cooked peas about 10 minutes before the cuttlefish has finished cooking.

The best part about cuttlefish-ink dishes is the big black smile people produce at the end of the meal, satisfied and unaware. Well, maybe not the best part, but a funny one nonetheless — and all the funnier after a couple of glasses of Soave, which happens to wash down seppie very well. I speak from experience here, following a long career in making a bad impression (most memorably on my wedding day).

Cuttlefish-ink-based dishes are some of the most talked-about Venetian specialities. They are intimidating at first, but rewarding for those who dare to attempt them. They usually take two forms: risotto and stew. Since two inky recipes seemed excessive, I thought to feature the stew. It's less well known than the inky risotto, but just as worthy of attention.

The concept is simple. Cuttlefish is cooked in a pitch-black sauce until butter-tender. The ink imparts not just a striking colour, but a nice earthy, briny note, too, enhancing the flavour of the fish. Served with soft white polenta, as tradition demands, it's a dish of great dignity, and one of the best representations of the cuisine of the Venetian lagoon.

Wash the cuttlefish under cold running water. Cut it into strips of about 5mm | ¼ inch and set aside.

Heat the oil in a heavy-based pan over a medium heat. Add the onion and fry gently until soft and translucent. Next, add the cuttlefish and fry for a couple of minutes, stirring often, until it turns opaque. Pour in the wine and allow it to evaporate before adding the tomato sauce and the stock. Reduce the heat to a simmer, cover and cook for about 30 minutes, or until the liquid has reduced to a thick sauce and the cuttlefish is extremely tender. Taste and adjust the seasoning.

Finally, in a small bowl, dissolve the ink sacs in 15 ml | 1 tablespoon of warm water; strain the ink and add it to the cuttlefish. Cook for 5 more minutes, stirring often, and then remove from the heat. Sprinkle with parsley and serve.

BRUSAOCI IN PAEA CO LA PANSETA
Stir-Fried Dandelion Leaves with Pancetta

BISI COL POMODORO
Peas in Red Sauce

SALSA DE MEANSANE
Aubergine Stew

POMODORI AJO E BASILICO
Tomatoes with Garlic & Basil

RADECI E FASOI
Borlotti Beans & Radicchio

VERZE SOFEGÀ
Braised Cabbage

PATATE TIPO PURÈ
Mashed Potatoes with Rosemary & Garlic

FASOI SCHICETI
Creamed Borlotti Beans

SEGOLETE IN DOLSEGARBO
Sweet & Sour Braised Baby Onions

CONTORNI

Stir-Fried Dandelion Leaves with Pancetta

SERVES 4

600g | 1lb 5oz dandelion
    leaves
60ml | ¼ cup extra virgin
    olive oil
70g | 2½oz piece of
    flat pancetta, cut into
    small cubes
2 garlic cloves, lightly crushed
Fine-grain sea salt

In Veneto, we call dandelions brusaoci. *The name literally means 'burn the eyes', perhaps alluding to the blinding colour of the flower. We also refer to them as* pissacàn, *an appellative suggesting that dogs like weeing on them. Either way, dandelions don't sound too inviting, but this doesn't stop us from collecting and eating them, and in large amounts, too.*

Dandelions emerge in early spring and are best caught right away, when the leaves are still tender and the flower hasn't formed. In the past, people used to blanch them quickly and then stir-fry them in the rendered fat of cooked salame, to which dandelions would be a side. That's exactly how my grandparents would enjoy these awfully bitter and yet strangely addictive leaves, granted that they always had some of their own fresh home-made salame on hand. These days, we make do with cubed pancetta.

Pancetta is a fine solution: it is fatty enough to dress the greens without taking anything away from their nice astringency. The fat leftover from frying sausages would work just as well here, as long as you eat the sausages with your greens for good measure.

Wash the dandelion leaves in plenty of cold water until the water runs clear. Pick them over and then spin dry in a salad spinner.

Bring a large pan of salted water to the boil. Drop in the dandelion leaves and blanch for 3 minutes. Drain, squeeze out any excess water and chop roughly.

Heat the oil in a large frying pan over a medium-high heat and cook the pancetta until it's nicely browned and crisp. Remove and set aside, leaving the melted fat in. Add the garlic and fry until fragrant but not browned. Next, throw in the dandelion leaves and stir-fry for 7–8 minutes, until softened and glistening with fat.

Finally, return the pancetta and then sauté everything for a couple of minutes. Remove from the heat and serve.

Peas in Red Sauce

SERVES 4

15ml | 1 tablespoon extra
   virgin olive oil
15g | 1 tablespoon
   unsalted butter
½ golden onion, chopped
350g | 2¾ cups fresh
   or frozen peas
2 teaspoons white wine
   vinegar
30g | 2 tablespoons
   tomato purée
1 teaspoon caster sugar
Fine-grain sea salt and freshly
   ground black pepper, to taste

Many recipes with peas appear in this book. I decided to keep them all because they are very much representative of the amount of peas we have always gone through in my family, in the old as much as in the new days, having had pea plants in our gardens for as long as we can recall.

In an attempt to use up our sizeable share, we ate peas in all fashions — tossed in sauces and soups (see Risi e Bisi *on page 53), braised in butter with bits of ham, or stewed with onion and tomato until wrinkly. This last way — peas in red sauce — is a family favourite. The recipe is simple and rather old-school, but it's lovely, and can be made ahead and in large batches, and even jarred, like Grandma does, for future use.*

I like pairing this saucy side with more saucy foods: Polpette al Sugo *(see page 202), or* Pollo in Tocio *(see page 70) would be my picks. In all cases, polenta or bread come handy to help collecting the delicious juices left on the plate at the end.*

Place the oil and butter in a medium pan over a medium heat. Add the onion and fry gently until soft and translucent. Add the peas and stir to coat them in fat. Allow them to cook for a couple of minutes, until they change their colour. Deglaze with the vinegar and let it evaporate. Add the tomato purée diluted in 4 tablespoons of water, plus the sugar.

Continue cooking, uncovered, until the peas are tender, a bit wrinkly even, and have absorbed all the water. Season, stir, cook for 1 more minute and then remove from the heat and serve.

Aubergine Stew

SERVES 6

5 large aubergines, trimmed
    and diced
2 large green peppers,
    deseeded, trimmed
    and diced
1 golden onion, diced
4 ripe San Marzano or vine
    tomatoes, deseeded
    and diced
90ml | 6 tablespoons
    extra virgin olive oil
Fine-grain sea salt

Note: The recipe doesn't
require any precision in dicing
the vegetables; imperfection is
actually encouraged here, as
slightly different sizes will give
way to a nice mix of textures —
part chunky and part creamy.

This summer stew is particularly popular in the Venetian countryside: it's a perfect way to use up wonky peppers and tomatoes past their prime, and it freezes well, too. Every household has its recipe, tricks and names. Some call it peperonata *(even though it's not). Grandma simply calls it* salsa.

In my family, there has always been a bit of competition between Grandma and Mum for the title of salsa *master. The two versions feature the same ingredients (aubergines, green peppers, onions, and tomatoes), which are grown in the same garden; and yet they are completely different. Grandma's is rich and glistening with oil, so much so that after eating only a few spoonfuls one needs a shot of* amaro, *and then a nap. Mum's, on the other hand, sees a lot less oil; it's a bit chunky and often 'smoky', particularly when she's busy reading and forgets to stir it.*

We like Mum's, but Grandma's is just too good to resist. Even Mum secretly prefers the rival's version; in fact, she loves it so much that she can be seen lunching on it alone, spoon in one hand and a piece of pan biscotto *in the other. Though, of course, she'd never admit it.*

———————

Put all the diced vegetables into a very large pan. Stir to create an even mix. Pour in the oil and stir once more.

Place over a very low heat and cook for 45–50 minutes, stirring occasionally, until you have a jammy, creamy mixture, ideally with some of the aubergine bits still holding their shape.

Once done, season with salt and stir again. Remove from the heat and allow to cool completely. Serve at room temperature, as a side or a starter, perhaps alongside some crunchy bread such as *pan biscotto*, crackers or *grissini*.

Tomatoes with Garlic & Basil

SERVES 4

5 medium bull's heart
  or beefsteak tomatoes,
  at room temperature

10 basil leaves

2 large garlic cloves, thinly
  sliced

45ml | 3 tablespoons extra
  virgin olive oil

Fine-grain sea salt, to taste

Every day in the summer Grandpa would eat a bowl of tomato salad. He would prepare it early in the morning and let it sit in lots of oil, garlic and torn basil until softened and flavoursome. He would only use produce from his garden, of course; as for tomatoes, only his bull's heart would do — meaty and with few seeds, they were perfect for salad.

He liked accompanying this with a big chunk of infamous Venetian bread — vaguely chalky and with lots of crumb, of the kind the door-to-door baker would deliver every day at midday. The meal couldn't start without bread because, of course, the tomato salad needed something to sup up the delicious juices left on the bottom of the bowl.

Whenever we make this salad at home, now, we follow Grandpa's example. First we ensure that we have bread for the juice mopping, and then, that we have enough time for the tomatoes to rest and soak up the flavour of the aromatics. Normally, we would serve it with fresh cheese such as mozzarella, ricotta, or local casatella. *Add a plate of* prosciutto e fichi *(see page 149) and a bowl of glistening green beans (see page 211) and you have my favourite summer feast.*

Not unlike the recipe for Spaghetti col Pomodoro Fresco *(see page 168), the success of this salad lies in the flavour of its ingredients — the tomatoes, certainly, but also the oil. Veneto has started to consume olive oil in recent times. In my family, for example, it wasn't really used until the first supermarkets arrived in town in the late 1980s. Grandpa did use it for his tomato salads, though he preferred the sort of light-tasting oil that suits a novice's palate. I, on the other hand, like my olive oil full-bodied, green, grassy and peppery, particularly when tomatoes are involved. Good mono-varietal oils from Umbria or Sicily are perfect here.*

Cut the tomatoes into wedges and place them in a salad bowl. Tear the basil leaves and scatter them on top. Add the sliced garlic, salt and finally the oil. Toss to dress evenly and leave to rest at room temperature for 1 hour before serving.

Borlotti Beans & Radicchio

SERVES 4

300g | 10½oz dried borlotti
    beans, soaked overnight

1 celery stick, trimmed and
    cut in half

½ carrot, peeled

½ golden onion

2 garlic cloves

2 bay leaves

60ml | ¼ cup extra virgin
    olive oil

1 sprig of rosemary

300g | 10½oz (about 1 large
    head) radicchio chioggiotto
    or trevisano

2 teaspoons white wine
    vinegar

Fine-grain sea salt and freshly
    ground black pepper, to taste

There are many versions of this iconic wintry side dish. The first, perhaps the most popular, is achieved by cooking and puréeing a good deal of borlotti beans, then mixing the purée with a bowlful of radicchio leaves as if it were a creamy dressing. The second is similar but calls for puréeing half of the cooked beans while leaving half of them intact. Another is actually a sort of thick bean soup where the radicchio leaves are used as a topping. And one last version wants the beans cooked al dente and tossed together with the radicchio into a salad of sorts.

This last take on the tradition is what we do at home. Dressed with a hit of vinegar, they are served as a side to chicken (see page 70) or cheesy polenta (see page 39).

As for the type of beans, dried borlotti from Lamon or Cuneo are excellent. They hold their shape well and have a nice nuttiness that balances out the bitterness of the radicchio.

Drain the beans and rinse them well under cold running water. Place them in a large pan together with the celery, carrot, onion, garlic and bay leaves and cover with double the volume of cold water. Place over a medium heat and bring to the boil. Cook for about 40 minutes, or until the beans are soft but still al dente, checking occasionally and skimming off any foam. When done, drain and discard the aromatics.

Heat half the olive oil in a large frying pan. Add the rosemary and allow it to infuse the oil for about 30 seconds before discarding. Add the beans, season with salt and pepper and sauté for 4–5 minutes over a medium-high heat. Remove and set aside.

Wash the radicchio and spin dry in a salad spinner. Tear the leaves and place them in a large salad bowl. Add the beans and mix. Make a dressing with the remaining oil, the vinegar and a pinch of salt. Pour it over the salad, toss to coat and serve.

Braised Cabbage

SERVES 4–6

45ml | 3 tablespoons extra
    virgin olive oil
1 golden onion, finely chopped
1kg | 2lb 3oz green cabbage,
    shredded
15ml | 1 tablespoon white
    wine vinegar
15g | 1 tablespoon tomato
    purée
Fine-grain sea salt and freshly
    ground black pepper, to taste

Note: The dish is even better
the second day, when flavours
have had the chance to set
and mingle. Once cooked, it
freezes well and reheats easily
in a pot with a thin layer of
water added.

Grandma has the power to turn every food she touches into something worthy of notice. Her range of action is fairly limited, but whatever she decides to tackle, she transforms into an instant classic. Take cabbage, for instance: it's hardly something to get excited about. And yet, her braised cabbage is pretty exciting, so much so that I'm always happy to dine on a massive plateful of it alone, accompanied by nothing more than crunchy bread (pan biscotto).

Tomato purée and vinegar are summoned once again (versatile, these two, aren't they?). The fact is that they work well with both meat and vegetables (and sometimes fish, too), and impart the sort of sauciness and sharpness that is often extremely pleasant. In this case, they give a hint of sourness to the sweet, caramelised cabbage that makes the dish vaguely Asian, and as such, definitely unique within the Venetian flavour spectrum.

Heat the oil in a large, heavy-based pan placed over a low heat. Add the onion and fry gently, stirring often, until very soft. Add the shredded cabbage and stir. Leave to sweat, covered, for about 5 minutes, stirring frequently. Now, pour in about 120ml water and cover with a lid.

Cook the cabbage for about 1 hour, or until extremely tender and almost falling apart. Check it every now and then, stir and add a little more water if needed.

Towards the end of the cooking, add the vinegar and tomato purée and season with salt and pepper. Stir to combine and then cook for 5 more minutes, until all the liquid has evaporated and the cabbage looks saucy. Taste and adjust the seasoning, then remove from the heat and let it sit for about 10 minutes before serving.

Mashed Potatoes with Rosemary & Garlic

SERVES 6

15ml | 1 tablespoon extra virgin olive oil

3 garlic cloves, very finely chopped

2kg | 4lb 6oz floury potatoes, peeled and thinly sliced

110g | ½ cup unsalted butter, diced

1 sprig rosemary, leaves picked and very finely chopped

Fine-grain sea salt and freshly ground black pepper, to taste

No Sunday lunch at Grandma's could ever go by without her serving her famous purè. *Who knows how she came up with this potato concoction, or where or from whom she got it. She doesn't seem to recall, and I suspect she just made it up. Just like her apple strudel, which has nothing in common with the real thing except for apples, her* purè *doesn't have anything to do with the classic* purè di patate *except for spuds.*

Admittedly, we all loved the 'fake purè' *so much that we didn't care about the details; what worried us more was the abundant dose of garlic that it contained, but only if we had to go somewhere later in the afternoon — the movies, say, or Mass. Anyway, it never seemed to be a sufficient deterrent, for the pot was regularly, unmistakably emptied and cleaned of every last bit of buttery potato scrumptiousness there was.*

Not unlike risotto, the final phase, in which the butter is added, will determine part of the texture. When stirring very fast, the fat whips and traps air bubbles, producing a fluffy, feathery mash that will feel much lighter than the sum of its parts.

Heat the oil in a large pan over a medium heat. Add the garlic and fry for a couple of minutes, until fragrant. Next, add the potatoes; cook them for 2–3 minutes, stirring often, then pour over 800ml | 3⅓ cups water. Bring to a simmer, then reduce the heat and cook, stirring frequently, until the water has evaporated and the potatoes have turned into mash. Taste and season generously.

Once done, remove from the heat and add the butter and chopped rosemary. Using a wooden spoon, stir the mash quickly and at length as if to 'whip' it. Taste and adjust the seasoning if needed. Serve.

Creamed Borlotti Beans

SERVES 4–6

600g | 1lb 5oz dried borlotti
  beans, soaked overnight
2 bay leaves
45g | 3 tablespoons lard,
  at room temperature
1 garlic clove, whole but
  lightly crushed
1 sprig of rosemary
Fine-grain sea salt and freshly
  ground black pepper, to taste

Note: This recipe suggests
the use of a food mill, which
purées the beans while
retaining part of the skins,
for a smoother result. If you
don't have one you can also
use a food processor, though
I encourage you to seek it
out — it makes a difference.
If you don't love the idea of
lard, substitute extra virgin
olive oil.

Borlotti beans feature heavily in this book, a testament to the crucial role they have always played in the cuisine of the Venetian inland. Beans combined with pasta or polenta constituted a cheap source of protein and energy for those who couldn't afford much meat in their diet. Whoever had a parcel of land would plant a few rows of borlotti, for they weren't difficult to grow and had a decent yield.

Beans were usually planted in May and harvested in August, under the dazzling summer sun, then dried in the farmyard and finally podded and stored in large wooden boxes for the rest of the year. The box was accessed on a daily basis, for the usual bean and pasta soup (see page 47) and for the occasional bean salad (see page 212), but also to make fasoi schiceti, *(literally, 'crushed beans') a lush bean purée laced with garlic and lard. The classic complement to these mashed beans would be grilled pancetta and/or sausages (see pages 76–77), and of course, grilled polenta, though they make a fairly nourishing meal on their own.*

Drain the beans and rinse them well under cold running water. Put them in a large pan together with the bay leaves and cover with double the volume of cold water. Place over a medium heat and bring to the boil. Cook the beans for about 45 minutes, or until very tender. Drain and discard the bay leaves.

Set a food mill over a bowl (see Note, left). Add the beans a handful at a time, and purée them, discarding any scraps. Once you've finished, pass them through a final time to make your purée extra smooth.

Heat the lard with the garlic and rosemary in a large heavy-based pan. Let them infuse the fat for a couple of minutes, making sure they don't burn, then discard them. Add the puréed beans and stir energetically. Taste and season with salt and pepper. Carry on cooking for 3–4 minutes, stirring often, then remove from the heat and serve.

Sweet & Sour Braised Baby Onions

SERVES 4–6

450g | 1lb baby onions, peeled
  (see Note below)
30ml | 2 tablespoons extra
  virgin olive oil
2 bay leaves
50g | ¼ cup granulated sugar
60ml | ¼ cup balsamic
  vinegar or red wine
Fine-grain sea salt, to taste

Note: Borrettane onions
from Emilia Romagna are
an excellent small variety,
sweet and versatile. Some
greengrocers sell them
ready-peeled, which is handy;
otherwise, put on some nice
music and be ready for a
cathartic cry.

Soft, juicy, messy and melting, braised baby onions are to boiled beef (see page 198) what cream is to crumble: the two should never be apart. The same could be said for aged cheese from Veneto, which pairs with these onions as if they were a chutney of sorts.

The Venetian recipe for cipolline *(yet another example of the Venetian love of* dolsegarbo, *see also* Sarde in Saor, *pages 27–28) — calls for wine vinegar. This produces a sweet and sour number in which the sour is so intense that it unclogs your nose. A version with balsamic vinegar, on the other hand, is less classic but more enjoyable — sticky, syrupy and outright irresistible. It's the method we follow at home, and I could not recommend it more.*

———————

Bring a large pan of salted water to the boil. Add the peeled baby onions and boil for 5 minutes, until just softened. Drain and set aside.

Next, heat the olive oil in a large heavy-based pan. Add the bay leaves and the onions and stir. Cook for 5 minutes — just enough for the onions to colour — then add the sugar and cover with about 360ml | 1½ cups of water. Reduce the heat and cover with a lid.

Cook for about 45 minutes, or until the liquid has reduced to a syrupy sauce and the onions are very tender. At this point, add the vinegar and season with salt. Stir gently to avoid breaking the onions and simmer for 10 more minutes, until the vinegar has evaporated.

Remove from the heat and leave to cool slightly before serving.

TIRAMISÙ
'Pick Me Up' Pudding

ZAETI (pictured)
Polenta Raisin Biscuits

PASTINE DE RISO
Rice Pudding Tartlets

PASQUALINA
Crumbly Easter Teacake

SBRISOLONA
Almond Polenta Shortbread Tart

PINZA VENETA
Polenta Cake with Dried Fruit

FRÌTOLE
Venetian-Style Doughnuts

FUGASSA DE POMI
Vintage Apple Cake

SÙGOI
Grape Must Pudding

DOLCI

TIRAMISÙ
'Pick Me Up' Pudding

SERVES 6–8

4 eggs, separated

60g | heaped ¼ cup caster sugar

500g | 1lb 2oz fresh mascarpone

60ml | ¼ cup whipping cream

360ml | 1½ cups strong brewed coffee, at room temperature

500g | 1lb 2oz *savoiardi* (ladyfingers)

10g | 2 tablespoons unsweetened dark cocoa powder

Tiramisù is easily the most exported Italian dessert. Many don't know that it was first devised in Treviso, at the restaurant Le Becchiere. A recent dispute between Veneto and Friuli Venezia Giulia has put a question mark on its actual authorship, stating that there are actually four original versions: two Venetian (from the Treviso area), and two from the neighbouring region, and that all are legit.

Whatever the answer, a few crucial points should be borne in mind when attempting tiramisù *at home. Good mascarpone is the first. Fresh hand-made artisan mascarpone does make a difference, but it's also hard to find, so any mascarpone is better than none. In case you can't find it at all, you can easily make it at home (See Note overleaf). Substituting it with ricotta, cream cheese or similar, on the other hand, is not appropriate.*

Another crucial point is the presence or absence of liqueur: purists say no booze, but it's ultimately up to you. If you like a drop of brandy in your coffee, go ahead. Biscuits: ladyfingers, nothing else. Finally, a word on the coffee: for tiramisù, *Italian-style percolated (Moka pot) coffee is best. A concentrated cafetière brew works, too, while filter or instant coffee won't stand up to the task.*

The recipe I'm sharing is for Mum's signature tiramisù — *a version that has always met with everybody's approval. With time and practice (she pulls it off pretty much any time pudding is required), she seems to have found a way to achieve the perfect ratio of cream to biscuits, with just enough coffee to make the biscuits soft but never stodgy. Her mascarpone cream, however heretical, is quite remarkable, too: whipped egg whites make it light, while a small dose of fresh whipped cream cuts through the egg flavour and gives freshness and a subtle milky note.*

CONTINUED OVERLEAF

Note: To make homemade mascarpone, bring 2 litres | 8⅓ cups of double cream to a simmer, stirring frequently to prevent it from scalding on the pan. Just before it boils, remove it from the heat and add 60ml | ¼ cup freshly squeezed and strained lemon juice. Allow the cream to cool and thicken for about 2 hours. After this, place a sieve over a bowl and line it with 3–4 layers of cheesecloth or muslin. Pour in the cream, then place everything in the fridge to drain for about 8 hours. Eventually, you should have a smooth, thick cream — that's your mascarpone. Keep refrigerated and use within 1 week.

In a large bowl, whisk the yolks with the sugar until creamy and pale yellow. Add the mascarpone and fold through until combined — a few lumps here and there are okay. In a separate bowl, whip the cream and then stir it into the mascarpone mixture. In a third bowl — ideally stainless steel or glass — whip the egg whites to stiff peaks. Add them to the mascarpone cream and fold through with gentle circular movements from the bottom to the top.

Take a square or rectangular high-sided glass dish about 30 × 23cm | 11 × 9 inches (or alternatively 1 large or 2 medium trifle bowls). Pour the coffee into a bowl. Dip the *savoiardi* in the coffee, moving quickly so that they don't soak up too much liquid and become mushy. Use them to line the dish, then cover them with one-third of the mascarpone cream, spreading it evenly and encouraging it to run down all sides and corners. Repeat with 2 more layers of biscuits alternated with mascarpone cream, finishing with a layer of cream.

Refrigerate the tiramisù for at least 6 hours, or preferably overnight. Serve chilled, with a light dusting of cocoa powder on top.

ZAETI
Polenta Raisin Biscuits

MAKES ABOUT 30

80g | ½ cup raisins
60ml | ¼ cup grappa (or use
 warm water)
280g | 2⅓ cups plain flour,
 sifted
250g | heaped 1½ cups fine
 polenta (such as Fioretto)
Pinch of fine-grain sea salt
½ teaspoon baking powder
180g | ⅔ cup + 2 tablespoons
 unsalted butter, chilled
 and diced
2 eggs, plus 2 egg yolks
½ teaspoon vanilla extract
150g | ⅔ cup caster sugar
Icing sugar, for dusting
 (optional)

Mum has always shown an allergy to baking, but she had a strange fondness for making zaeti — the cute Venetian biscuits made with polenta and raisins. Mind you, she didn't indulge in this activity very often. But if she had people over for coffee and couldn't be bothered to swing past the bakery, she would make an exception, pull out the paper scrap with the scribbled recipe, and fire up the oven.

Zaeti (also zaleti *or* zaletti *in dialect, and* gialletti *in Italian) are traditionally bound to the carnival festivities. These days you can find them all year round in cafés, pastry shops and bakeries all over Venice and the Venetian inland. It's not uncommon to see them on the dessert list in local* osterie *and restaurants, to be eaten with a glass of Moscato or Malvasia.*

Soak the raisins in grappa or warm water for 20 minutes, then drain and pat dry with kitchen paper. Set aside.

In a large bowl, combine the flour, polenta, salt and baking powder. Add the butter and work it into the flour mix using the tips of your fingers until you have a crumbly, coarse, sandy mixture. In a separate bowl, whisk the eggs and yolks with the vanilla and sugar until frothy and pale yellow. Fold them gently into the flour mix until the dough comes together. Stir in the raisins and mix to combine. Cover the bowl with cling film and place it in the fridge to cool for 1 hour.

Preheat the oven to 180°C | 350°F | gas mark 4 and line 2 baking sheets with parchment. Take a roughly tablespoon-sized piece of dough and shape it into an oval using your hands. Ease it onto the prepared sheet and press it down gently. Repeat with the rest of the dough, making sure to space out the biscuits.

Bake for 20 minutes, or until golden and lightly cracked on top but still rather soft within (shift the trays halfway through so that they bake evenly). Remove from the oven and transfer the biscuits to a wire rack to cool. Once cooled, dust with icing sugar if you wish. Store in an airtight container for up to 2 weeks.

Rice Pudding Tartlets

MAKES 12

For the rice pudding:

1 litre | 4¼ cups whole milk

75g | ⅓ cup caster sugar

Zest of ½ unwaxed
   lemon, stripped with
   a vegetable peeler

Pinch of fine-grain sea salt

½ vanilla pod, slit lengthways
   and seeds scraped out
   (optional)

150g | ¾ cup pudding or
   risotto rice

For the custard:

2 egg yolks

55g | ¼ cup caster sugar

20g | 3 tablespoons
   cornflour, sifted

240ml | 1 cup whole milk

Zest of ½ unwaxed
   lemon, stripped with
   a vegetable peeler

For the pastry:

250g | 2 cups + 1 tablespoon
   plain flour, sifted, plus more
   for dusting

110g | 1 cup icing sugar, plus
   more for dusting

125g | ½ cup + 1 tablespoon
   unsalted butter, chilled and
   cut into small cubes, plus
   more for the tin

1 egg plus 1 yolk, lightly
   beaten

A tray of pastine *from the nearby pastry shop was a regular presence on Grandma's Sunday table. We all knew the ritual. At the end of the meal, Aunt would stand up, open the fridge and announce, rather loudly, that she had bought some* pastine. *Grandpa, who was already snoozing in front of his emptied plate, would wake up uttering some muffled imprecation. Dad, full to the brim with roast and potatoes, would look vaguely disconcerted. The only enthusiastic people in the room would be my brother and I (and Grandma): the best part of the meal had come.*

Picking the right pastina *is no laughing matter — particularly, if you only get to eat one. The choice requires some careful assessment of the virtues of the chocolate* bigné *versus the deliciousness of the hazelnut biscuit, of the glories of the* cannoncino *(a cone of puff pastry stuffed with vanilla custard) against the fruit* tartelette. *Options assessed, I would always pick the same: the unbeatable, the one and only* pastina di riso.

Pastine di riso (also called risini *in Verona), consist of a dollop of custardy rice pudding baked in a shell of sugar pastry. Many pastry shops and bakeries offer them, but they are rewarding to make at home, too, whenever you're in the mood for a relaxing three-step project and some nostalgic baking.*

Place the milk, sugar, strips of lemon zest, salt and the scraped vanilla seeds, if using, in a pan and set it over a medium heat. Bring to the boil, then remove the lemon zest and add the rice. Reduce the heat to a simmer and cook for 45–50 minutes, or until the rice is very soft and has absorbed all the liquid, stirring very often. Remove from the heat and set aside to cool.

CONTINUED OVERLEAF

Next, make the custard. Beat the egg yolks with half of the sugar until frothy and pale yellow. Add the cornflour and whisk to incorporate, then pour in 60ml | ¼ cup of the milk in a thin stream, whisking all the while, until you have a smooth, clump-free batter. Set aside. Heat the remaining milk in a small pan together with the rest of the sugar and strips of lemon zest. Moments before the milk begins to boil, remove it from the heat and strain it. Pour it in a thin stream into the bowl with the egg batter, whisking energetically all the while. Pour this mixture back in a clean pan and set it over a low heat. Cook the custard until thickened, stirring continuously. Transfer to a glass bowl, cover the surface directly with cling film and set over an ice bath to cool.

Now, prepare the pastry. Combine the flour and sugar in a large bowl. Rub the butter into the flour using the tips of your fingers until you have a coarse, crumbly mix. Add the egg and the yolk, and knead until the dough comes together into a smooth ball — try not to overwork it. Wrap it in cling film and leave it to rest in the fridge for 30 minutes.

When everything is cooled and rested, preheat the oven to 180°C | 350°F | gas mark 4. Roll the pastry into a circle that is 2mm thick and large enough to line 12 × 9.5cm | 3½-inch tartlet tins (or a 12-hole muffin tin; the holes should be about 7cm | 2¾ inches in diameter) dusting your work surface and moving/ turning the dough often so it doesn't stick to it. Lightly grease the tartlet tins or holes with butter. Cut the pastry into circles and use to line the tins, pressing lightly with your fingertips to make it stick. Cut off any excess pastry. Stir together the rice pudding and the custard and use to fill the lined tins to the top.

If you are using muffin tins, set them side-by-side on the middle shelf of the oven. If you're using tartlet tins, place them on a baking sheet and set it on the middle shelf, too. Bake for 30–40 minutes (the muffins will take about 10 minutes less than the tartlets), or until the pastry is golden and the filling is set. Remove from the oven and allow them to cool in their tins. When at room temperature, unmould them carefully and dust with icing sugar.

PASQUALINA
Crumbly Easter Teacake

MAKES 1 / SERVES 6–8

300g | 2½ cups plain flour,
    sifted
2 teaspoons baking powder
Pinch of fine-grain sea salt
2 eggs
100g | ½ cup granulated
    sugar, plus more for
    sprinkling
100g | ⅓ cup + 1½
    tablespoons unsalted butter,
    melted and cooled
Finely grated zest of
    2 unwaxed lemons
Milk, for brushing

As a young spouse and mother living with her husband and in-laws on their family farm, Grandma had to work her share in the kitchen. Baking bread was only one of her countless culinary chores. There wasn't an oven at their farm, only a cucina economica *(a wood-fire stove, that is) for soups, stews and other stovetop concoctions. Baking was done in bulk, twice a month, at the communal bakery next to the village mill. Wood and flour supplies were carried individually, so Grandma had to load her bicycle with a fortress of flour and branches and push it all for six miles, all the way to the mill.*

Baking took the best part of a day. It wasn't work for the faint of heart, as lots of heavy lifting and kneading went into it; though the reward would come eventually, in the form of many bread rolls, sturdy loaves, and a few bagfuls of dry, crisp pan biscotto*. The day would usually wrap up there, but at times, depending on the time of year (religious festivals particularly), Grandma enjoyed shovelling a small batch of something sweet in the cooling oven. They were rustic preparations, requiring little more than a handful of sugar and a couple of eggs, but these were precious ingredients, especially in times of war. And so, for All Saints Day, she would bake metres of friable flatbread seasoned with lard and studded with raisins and* ciccioli *(fried pork skins); for Christmas,* pagnocchelle *(a sort of soft bun) with raisins and bits of cooked polenta kneaded into the lightly sweetened dough; and for Easter, a bike-load of crumbly, sugar-topped* pasqualine *to donate to visiting relatives and neighbours who had less than she, or nothing at all.*

Many years have passed and the ritual of baking pasqualine *remains a cherished moment in our family. It is a tradition that Grandma, now in her mid-nineties, still fulfils by making enough cakes for all her children and their children, and all her neighbours for good measure. Now that she has an oven of her own, and no shortage of eggs and sugar, she enjoys baking them in the comfort of her solitary kitchen in the basement — her favourite place to retreat — kneading this massive amount of dough with almost as much energy as she used to have when she was young.*

CONTINUED OVERLEAF

Somewhere between a scone and a teacake, pasqualina *is a rather modest, subdued thing. What makes it special, besides its story, is the intense citrus note. The generous dose of lemon zest gives it assertiveness, turning what might seem like a big dense lump into a bright, crumbly, zingy affair. It's especially lovely when still warm, served for afternoon tea, or at the end of the meal with some sweet Malvasia. I also like dunking it in my breakfast coffee, particularly when the cake is a couple of days old.*

Preheat the oven to 180°C | 350°F | gas mark 4.

On a work surface, combine the flour with the baking powder and salt. Make a well and break the eggs in its centre; add the sugar and, using a fork, mix it with the eggs. Next, incorporate the flour, a little at the time, moving from the edges towards the centre. The mixture will soon start to assume a sort of scrambled-egg appearance. Make a new well in the middle and add the melted butter and grated lemon zest and work them into the dough until it comes together to form a ball.

Transfer the dough to a baking tray lined with parchment. Press it down lightly to flatten it. Inscribe a cross on the surface, brush with a bit of milk and sprinkle with sugar.

Bake for 25–30 minutes, or until a toothpick inserted into the centre of the cake comes out clean. Remove from the oven and leave to cool slightly on a wire rack before slicing and serving.

Almond Polenta Shortbread Tart

MAKES 1 / SERVES 8

100g | heaped ¾ cup plain
    flour, sifted

100g | ⅔ cup fine polenta
    (such as Fioretto)

100g | scant ½ cup caster
    sugar, plus more for
    sprinkling

Pinch of fine-grain sea salt

Finely grated zest of
    1 unwaxed lemon

100g | ⅓ cup + 1½
    tablespoons unsalted
    butter, softened, plus
    more for the tin

1 egg yolk

100g | ½ cup whole
    skin-on almonds
    (or use 50g | ¼ cup
    almonds and 50g |
    ¼ cup whole hazelnuts)

This brittle, buttery tart — a giant shortbread of sorts — originates from Mantua, in Lombardy. The reason why it found its way into a Venetian cookbook is, well, mostly because I love it. The second reason is proximity: Mantua is only a few miles from the border of Veneto. The area shares a similar landscape and a culinary repertoire to that of its neighbouring region, with constant cultural-culinary exchanges happening between the two.

Literally meaning 'big crumbly one', sbrisolona is a tart of humble provenance. Its modest ingredients consist of nothing more than polenta, flour, butter, sugar and just one precious egg. Hazelnuts were included in the original recipe, but modern adaptations call for almonds.

Sbrisolona is extremely simple to recreate at home. Traditionally served in chunks at the end of the meal, with coffee or grappa (or coffee 'corrected' with grappa), sbrisolona is equally good on its own or with a dollop of mascarpone cream. If you feel like embracing the Italian habit of eating biscuits for breakfast, this tart serves the purpose well, whether dipped in a steamy cup of caffelatte or crumbled in a bowl of cold milk and enjoyed like the sweetest of morning cereal.

In a large bowl, combine the flour, polenta, sugar, salt and lemon zest. Using your fingers, work the butter and the egg yolk into the flour mix until you have a coarse, crumbly mixture. Add the almonds and knead them in.

Grease a 23cm | 9-inch tart tin with butter. Lay the crumbs in the tin evenly and press them down lightly to make them stick to each other and the tin, but without flattening them — the surface should be craggy rather than smooth. Wrap in cling film and refrigerate for 1 hour.

Preheat the oven to 160°C | 320°F | gas mark 3. Bake the tart for 40 minutes, or until deep golden on the surface. Sprinkle with sugar and bake for a further 10 minutes. Remove from the oven and allow to cool completely before serving, broken into chunks.

PINZA VENETA
Polenta Cake with Dried Fruit

MAKES 2 / SERVES 8–10

100g | ⅓ cup + 1½
    tablespoons unsalted butter,
    melted, plus more for the tin
50g | ⅓ cup raisins
60ml | ¼ cup grappa
    (or use rum)
250g | heaped 1½ cups fine
    polenta (such as Fioretto)
100g | heaped ¾ cup
    plain flour
Pinch of fine-grain sea salt
1 litre | 4¼ cups whole milk
100g | scant ½ cup
    caster sugar
50g | ¼ cup whole, skin-on
    almonds, roughly chopped
60g | 2oz walnuts,
    roughly chopped
40g | ¼ cup pine nuts
60g | ⅓ cup candied citrus
    peel, very finely chopped
75g | 2½oz dried figs,
    roughly chopped
1 teaspoon fennel seeds
½ teaspoon ground cinnamon
⅛ teaspoon ground nutmeg
Finely grated zest of
    1 unwaxed lemon

Pinza is a Venetian term used to describe a range of cakes that are traditional to the region. All pinze *share the same humble origins — they are perfect examples of a poor man's cake — and all are laced with dried fruits, spices and other storecupboard scraps; some are made with day-old bread soaked in milk, others with leftover polenta, others again with a sort of rice pudding, and so on. They often include nuts, too, and depending on the time of the year, apples, pumpkin, or even sweet potato.*

The classic pinza *for Epifania (Three Kings' Day) entails polenta cooked in milk, then sprinkled with fennel seeds and as many dried fruits and nuts as one can find. The texture is soft, but it's played off nicely by the crunchiness of the nuts and the chewiness of the fruit. Fennel seeds give it a pleasant aromatic note, while the polenta makes it rustic and wholesome. It is traditionally paired with mulled wine or grappa as a mid-afternoon snack.*

Preheat the oven to 180°C | 350°F | gas mark 4 and grease 2 × 23cm | 9-inch square tins (or 2 equivalent tart tins) with butter.

Soak the raisins in grappa for 20 minutes. In a small bowl, combine the polenta with the flour and salt. Bring the milk to a simmer in a large pan, and when hot, slowly add the flours, whisking continuously to avoid clumps. Set the heat to medium-low and cook the flours for 15 minutes, until you have a thick polenta. Remove from the heat, add the melted butter and sugar and stir to combine. Add the rest of the ingredients, including the raisins and their grappa.

Transfer to the prepared tins and spread the mixture to 3cm | 1¼ inches thick, using your fingers to even out the surface. Bake for 30 minutes, then cover with foil and carry on cooking for a further 30 minutes. The cake is done when the surface becomes slightly wrinkly and the edges detach from the sides of the tin.

Allow to cool completely before cutting into pieces and serving.

Venetian-Style Doughnuts

MAKES ABOUT 15 LARGE
OR 25 SMALL DOUGHNUTS

150g | 1 cup raisins

120ml | ½ cup grappa
(see Note overleaf)

400g | 3⅓ cups plain
flour, sifted

10g | 3¼ teaspoons
fast-action dried yeast

100g | ½ cup granulated
sugar, plus more for rolling

Pinch of fine-grain sea salt

2 eggs, lightly beaten

160ml | ⅔ cup whole milk,
lukewarm, or as needed

40g | ¼ cup pine nuts,
lightly toasted

Finely grated zest of
1 unwaxed lemon

60g | ⅓ cup candied citrus
peel (optional)

Sunflower oil, for frying

The big Venetian carnival fry-up plot unfolds every year in a similar way. On the night before Shrove Tuesday/Mardi Gras, the phone rings. It's Grandma. She's made frìtole, *she says, screaming into the receiver as usual, sure that I'll hear her better if she does. 'Can you come and pick them up?' she asks. I look outside: it's a gloomy, wet, foggy February night; but then again, yes, I could make the effort for a bowl of doughnuts. I bundle up and go out.*

Grandma lives down the road from us, a one-minute walk door to door. I find her downstairs, as always when she's spent the whole day cooking. She's busy cleaning up, traces of sugar on the floor. The air is filled with a biting scent, a mix of yeast and exhausted frying oil. On the table are three small platoons of aluminium trays neatly covered with flowery kitchen paper. She grabs a tray from each group and presses them into my hands: one filled with paper-thin squares (crostoli); *one with walnut-sized balls* (favette), *and one with a pile of spongy, pillowy* frìtole.

'I thought you just made frìtole?'
'Yes, well, since I had the oil going . . . '

Venetians are religious about their Carnival. It's a century-old recurrence that can't be ignored, not just in the city but in the countryside, too. Kids dress up and parade, and everybody stuffs their faces with fried treats. I like the Carnival triplet of crostoli, favette *and* frìtole *(or* frittelle), *and I like that Grandma has taken on the chore of frying up a storm for the whole family, year in and year out. Of the three,* frìtole *are her strongest — soft, perfumed with anise and citrus, and surprisingly un-greasy. I'm happy to be sharing her recipe here.*

CONTINUED OVERLEAF

Note: Some like using anise liqueur instead of grappa for soaking the raisins: it'll definitely increase the aromatic potential of these *frìtole*, though you must like anise in the first place. Candied citrus peel and pine nuts are often omitted in traditional recipes, while raisins are often present: my suggestion would be to find the combination you like the best.

Soak the raisins in grappa and let them plump up for 20 minutes, then drain well and set aside.

In a large bowl, combine the flour, yeast, sugar and salt. Add the eggs and lukewarm milk and work them into the dry ingredients. Next stir in the raisins, pine nuts, grated lemon zest and candied citrus peel, if using. Knead the dough until it looks even, elastic and smooth (add a little more milk if it appears too dry; it should be fairly sticky). Cover with a clean tea towel and leave to rise in a dry, warm place for about 2 hours, or until it has doubled in volume and the surface is full of tiny bubbles.

Fill two-thirds of a medium, high-sided frying pan with sunflower oil. Place it over a medium heat and wait until it reaches a temperature of 180°C | 350°F, which you can test with a thermometer or by inserting the handle of a wooden spoon in the oil; when small but fierce bubbles form around the handle, it's ready. Using 2 tablespoons, grab a spoonful of dough and slide it into the hot oil. Fry 6-7 *frìtole* at a time, turning with a slotted spoon, until dark brown on all sides. Drain with the slotted spoon and transfer to a large plate covered with kitchen paper.

Leave the *frìtole* to cool slightly before rolling them in plenty of granulated sugar. Enjoy them warm or within 12 hours of frying.

Vintage Apple Cake

MAKES 1 / SERVES 8

125g | ½ cup + 1 tablespoon
   unsalted butter, melted and
   cooled, plus more for the tin
300g | 2½ cups plain flour,
   plus more for the tin
3 eggs
150g | ⅔ cup caster sugar
120ml | ½ cup whole milk
2 teaspoons baking powder
Pinch of fine-grain sea salt
Finely grated zest and juice
   of 1 unwaxed lemon
2 large Golden Delicious
   apples, cored, peeled
   and thinly sliced
Icing sugar, for dusting
   (optional)

Any Italian will tell you that they grew up eating home-made apple cake for breakfast or la merenda, *the afternoon snack. So will I. Grandma calls hers* fugassa, *because it's soft like a* focaccia. *The hefty dose of eggs makes it airy, but substantial, while the apples give it a semblance of wholesomeness that allows for second helpings.*

Golden Delicious is the apple of choice for many Italian nonne. *They appear to have the perfect texture for the task — neither hard nor floury nor mealy — and just the right dose of juiciness and sugar. Some excellent ones come to Veneto from the valleys of Trentino, but Grandma always preferred to buy them from the fruit grower down the road; he'd always throw a couple more in her bag for free, enough to make her happy.*

Preheat the oven to 180°C | 350°F | gas mark 4. Butter and flour a 20cm | 8-inch springform cake tin and set aside.

In a medium bowl, beat the eggs with the sugar until airy and pale yellow. Add the melted butter and the milk and whisk to combine. In a separate, large bowl, mix the flour, baking powder and salt. Pour the wet mixture over the flour mix; add the lemon zest and strained juice and a third of the apple slices, and fold through until combined.

Pour the batter into the prepared cake tin. Arrange the remaining apple slices on top. Set the cake on the middle shelf of the oven and bake for 50–55 minutes, or until the top is springy and deeply golden and a toothpick inserted into the centre of the cake comes out clean. If towards the end you notice that the apple slices are burning, cover with a piece of foil.

Remove the cake from the oven and allow it to cool in the tin for 10 minutes or so, then run a knife all around the edges and free the cake. Transfer it to a wire rack and leave to cool completely before dusting with icing sugar.

Grape Must Pudding

SERVES 4–6

1.5kg | 3lb 5oz red wine
  grapes (see Note below)
60ml | ¼ cup cold water
30g | ¼ cup cornflour, sifted
15g | 1 tablespoon caster
  sugar (optional, depending
  on the sweetness of
  the grapes)

Notes: Choose sweet wine
grapes such as Muscat,
Sangiovese or Concord for
this pudding: their natural
sugariness and intense colour
is key to the success of the
recipe.

Optional toppings include
cinnamon or dark cocoa
powder, though we never
used them in our home.

In rural Veneto, grapes have long been an accessible fruit. Even the poorest of seasonal workers, especially if enrolled in the vendemmia *(the grape harvest), was able to take some home to eat and cook with.*

Many of the women in my family, grape pickers themselves, found a way to make the most of these free fruits by turning them into a soft, jelly-like pudding called sùgoi. *Made with nothing more than grape juice (or 'must') and a bit of flour or cornflour,* sùgoi *was indeed the pudding of the humble farmworker. In modern times, this translates into a dessert that is simple and refreshing, and in which the natural sweetness of the grapes can really shine through.*

Wash the grapes and place them with the water in a large pan set over a medium heat. Bring to a simmer and cook until the grapes have burst and released their juice — use a wooden spoon to squeeze them.

Transfer to a fine-mesh sieve set over a bowl and strain the juice — move the skins around to get the most out of them. Or, use a food mill.

Pour the juice (must) back into the same pan and whisk in the flour or cornflour, plus the sugar, if using. Bring everything to a simmer over a low heat, whisking all the while. Cook the pudding until smooth, thick and creamy.

Remove from the heat and spoon into 4–6 serving cups. Allow the pudding to cool to room temperature before covering and chilling it in the fridge for at least 1 hour. Serve chilled.

In this section, you'll find recipes gathered from a wide range of sources. Some draw from childhood, and have subsequently become staples in my own kitchen. Others have been collected throughout the years I lived away from home. And others again (particularly in the antipasti section) were sparked by the many visits I paid to the wine bars of Venice and Padua. The thread that connects them all is, first, the frequency with which they appear on our table; but also their fresh flair (particularly when compared to the heartier recipes of the first section), and, lastly, their Venezianity *at heart.*

PART II

Now

Inspired Recipes from a
Modern Venetian Kitchen

For years, I had mixed feelings towards the tiny village where I grew up. Things are different now — it's where I long to be more than I care to admit — but my teenage self couldn't wait to run away. And so I did. I moved to Padua as soon as I finished high school and started university. I got a room, a bike and an invisible shield to screen the snarky comments of those back in the village who thought it was too close to justify not commuting. Padua is most certainly not a metropolis — I love the fact that one could bike anywhere in 20 minutes — but back then, it had everything I had ever wanted: young people, shops, bars, a flourishing daily market walking distance from my flat, and a (shared) kitchen where I could cook whatever I fancied.

I was too busy living to worry much about cooking at first, especially just for myself, but it soon became clear that I cared more than the average student. I took great pleasure in shopping for food. I bought from the stalls that the locals seemed to trust as having the nicest (though not the cheapest) seasonal produce. Using my tiny weekly budget, I would buy lots of fruits and vegetables to mix with a few nice staples (rice, bread, tinned anchovies, cheese)

from the established delicatessen tucked under the arches of the imposing Palazzo della Ragione, all to the detriment of my partying allowance. Back in my shared flat's kitchen, I would whip up simple meals inspired mostly by what I used to eat at home: rice and peas, rice and pumpkin, risotto (I ate a lot of rice!), minestrone, and then pasta with tomato sauce in summer, and big salads of radicchio and fennel in winter. Nothing fancy, really, but all pretty good nonetheless.

Food slowly became an interest, then a passion, and eventually a healthy obsession, but not without a little help from some serendipitous encounters. First up, my flat-mate Paolo, an avid cook and generous host who would always make an extra bowl of pasta for whoever was around, and whose mum would spoil us with her ridiculously good jams and pickled white asparagus. Then, my other flat-mate, Sari, son of butchers and a greens-hater: he never seemed to mind sharing his fantastic home-made salame with us. And finally, my classmate Chiara, from the hills of Valdobbiadene, who showed up at parties with a bottle of crown-capped prosecco from her dad's cellar, and presented me with green asparagus from her garden — the juiciest and snappiest I have ever tasted. These people, consciously or not, left a mark. They made me realise, too, that my true passion lay in cooking, eating and sharing dishes as much as stories, and told me that it was time for me to embrace it.

I moved from Padua to Piedmont with a car half-filled with Grandma's provisions and settled in a town called Bra, in the picturesque hills of Langhe, to take a masters in food culture at the prestigious University of Gastronomic Sciences. To me, that was *it* — it wasn't going to get any better than that. And in a way, I wasn't completely wrong. The masters course taught me a lot about culture and food and how to talk about it and taste it, but, in case you're wondering, it did not teach me a single thing about cooking (I remain very much the home cook whose knife skills are, at best, amateurish). But masters aside, those two years turned out to be dramatically life-changing for a number of reasons. For starters, it's where I met my future husband. But it's also where I had the chance to meet many like-minded people from all over the world, people who, like me, didn't mind spending a whole day talking about food, or nerding

out about fermentation, or being really picky about their cheese. I felt understood, enriched by other students' stories and, in turn, inspired to tell mine. And so, by means of many conversations and impromptu home-cooked meals, and by seeing myself through their eyes, I consolidated who I was as a cook and as a person. I was the Venetian. I cooked Venetian food.

This understanding and sense of self helped me a lot in my transition from the Italian countryside to a foreign city. In the four years I have lived in London, my way of cooking and eating has adapted ever so slightly to the availability of ingredients and the new speed of life, but the substance hasn't changed: seasonal ingredients and Venetian flavours have remained the focus of my cooking. It became evident that no matter how far I ran away from that village in the middle-of-nowhere-Veneto, I would never be able to shake off my identity as a person and as a cook; my cooking would always be bound to my Venetian roots. And in the end, I am glad this bond exists, because it was through food that I came to truly appreciate the place I'm from.

———————

SPRITZ AL CYNAR
Spritz, Padua-Style

CROSTINI CON SGOMBRO E CIPOLLINE
Mackerel & Pickled Onion Crostini

MEZZO UOVO CON L'ACCIUGA
Hard-Boiled Eggs with Anchovies

POLPETTE DI CARNE
Deep-Fried Shredded Beef Rissoles

POLPETTE DI BACCALĀ
Deep-Fried Cod Rissoles

PROSCIUTTO E FICHI
Prosciutto & Figs

ZUCCA IN SAOR
*Fried Marinated Pumpkin with
Onion, Pine Nuts & Raisins*

CAPESANTE GRATINATE CON MANDORLE E ARANCIA
Scallop Gratin with Almonds & Orange

CAPELONGHE CON AGLIO E PREZZEMOLO
Razor Clams with Garlic & Parsley

ANTIPASTI

SPRITZ AL CYNAR
Spritz, Padua-Style

MAKES 1

4–5 ice cubes
45ml | 3 tablespoons Aperol
45ml | 3 tablespoons Cynar
120ml | ½ cup prosecco,
  ideally Prosecco DOCG,
  chilled
Splash of seltzer or soda
  water, chilled
1 orange slice
1 Cerignola olive (optional)

If you've never tried making Venetian spritz at home, summer is the best time to start. Highly refreshing, mildly bitter and excellent for quenching some serious thirst, spritz is one of the easiest drinks ever invented. It is even more welcome at the end of a warm day, when you're chilling in the garden as the sun sets behind the houses.

Rumour has it that the first spritz was a light sparkler of white wine and sparkling water, devised by a group of Austrian soldiers campaigning in north-eastern Italy in an attempt to reduce the alcohol content of Italian wines. Today, the name is more commonly associated with the blushed, bittersweet beverage of worldwide fame — a mix of bitter liqueur, prosecco and seltzer. Veneto (Padua, in particular) is where this evolution took place.

Living in Padua for a few years as a student, I have drunk my fair share of spritz. My all-time favourite remains the spritz served at the infamous and picturesque Bar dei Osei — a hole in the wall tucked under the arches of the magnificent Palazzo della Ragione, in the heart of the city. Their spritz della casa, made with part Aperol and part Cynar, has a strikingly refreshing bitterness that is more pronounced than your usual spritz. It's a twist on the classic that I'm sure will appeal to anyone who, like me, has a bit of a bitter tooth.

Fill a tumbler with ice cubes. Pour in the Aperol and Cynar and top with prosecco and soda water. Stir well. Serve with the orange slice and, if liked, the olive, pierced with a skewer.

CROSTINI CON SGOMBRO E CIPOLLINE
Mackerel & Pickled Onion Crostini

SERVES 6

200g | 7oz (drained weight)
skinless and boneless
mackerel fillets in
extra virgin olive oil
(see Note below)

30g | 2½ tablespoons
mayonnaise

1 tablespoon finely chopped
flat-leaf parsley leaves

Freshly ground black pepper

18 slices of crusty baguette,
1cm | ½ inch thick

9 sweet pickled baby onions,
halved (or use 36 pickled
pearl-sized onions)

Note: It is important to choose
mackerel preserved in extra
virgin olive oil as opposed
to just olive oil — the two
differ dramatically in quality
and flavour. As for the baby
onions, the recipe on page 265
describes how to pickle them
in-house if you wish to give
it a go.

Walk inside any wine bar in Venice and you'll likely be faced with a cabinet filled with all manners of tempting savoury snacks. The snacking art is particularly refined in Venice, where colourful cicchetti *(from 'ciccus', or small) are consumed on a daily basis. Among the many bite-sized delights on offer, crostini are by far the most popular.*

The concept is simple: circles of bread with various toppings. Variations on the theme are potentially endless: one could easily hop from one bar to the other and taste something different every time. There are, of course, a few recurrent flavours, mostly linked to traditional recipes: baccalà mantecato *(see pages 21–22) and* lardo *on polenta (see page 36) come to mind first.*

I'd be hard pressed to pick a favourite crostino. I like them all. I wanted, however, to choose one that would feel both unique and representative of the Venetian crostini category. Mackerel and pickled onion ticks both boxes: preserved fish is a classic, mackerel is local to the Adriatic and sweet and sour pickled onions are always a good idea.

The combination impressed me when I first tasted it in a scruffy wine bar in Venice, and by the time I left I was already thinking of reproducing it at home. The ingredients couldn't be easier to source: just some crusty baguette (not indigenous but suited to the scope), a couple of tins of quality mackerel packed in extra virgin olive oil, and a jar of sweet and sour baby onions, and you're all set.

In a medium bowl, mash the mackerel with the mayonnaise. Add the parsley and pepper and stir to combine. Spoon the mixture onto the bread slices (you can toast them before or not, it's up to you; in Venice you'll find both). Top with half a pickled baby onion or 2 pearl-sized onions and serve.

Hard-Boiled Eggs with Anchovies

SERVES 4

4 eggs
8 oil-packed anchovy fillets,
    drained
2 teaspoons finely chopped
    flat-leaf parsley leaves
Fine-grain sea salt and freshly
    ground black pepper, to taste

Perhaps one of the most classic Venetian cicchetti, *hard-boiled eggs with anchovies can be found in the majority of* bàcari *(Venetian wine bars) around town. When you order one, you'll be handed exactly that: half a cooked egg with a toothpick piercing through an oil-coated anchovy. It might look unassuming, and it is. But in its unfussiness, it makes for the perfect mouthful, the creamy sweetness of the egg playing off the assertive flavour of the anchovy.*

One of the best reasons to give these a try, aside from the fact that they are silly easy and plain delicious in their simplicity, is that you can adjust the doneness of the egg according to your liking. My preference goes towards a creamy-hearted yolk; for a firmer set, add a couple of minutes to the suggested cooking time.

With such a short ingredients list, quality is key. For this, it's worth splurging on the best eggs and — especially — the best anchovies you can find. I like anchovies from Cetara, in Campania, but Spanish ones are good, too.

Place the eggs in a small pan filled with cold water and bring to the boil. As soon as it starts boiling, remove from the heat, cover with a lid and set a timer for 7 minutes. Drain and cool under cold running water.

Once lukewarm, peel and cut the eggs in half. Arrange on a plate and season with salt and pepper. Ease an anchovy fillet over each egg half and finish with a sprinkling of parsley.

Deep-Fried Shredded Beef Rissoles

MAKES 18–20

200g | 7oz (about 1 small)
  floury potato

80g | 2¾oz crustless
  white bread

60ml | ¼ cup whole milk

400g | 14oz boiled beef
  (prepared following the
  recipe on page 198),
  finely shredded

100g | 3½oz thick slice of
  sopressa or other Italian
  salami (see page 35), minced

1 egg, lightly beaten

1 garlic clove, very finely
  chopped

2 tablespoons very finely
  chopped flat-leaf
  parsley leaves

100g | 1 cup fine dry
  breadcrumbs

Fine-grain sea salt and freshly
  ground black pepper, to taste

Sunflower oil, for frying

The concept of recupero *is at the base of many traditional Venetian recipes.* Recuperare *means to retrieve, recover, recuperate; but also to reuse, repurpose, recycle. In food terms, it stands for fitting leftovers into a new recipe and finding creative ways to make it look different from what it once was, while remaining just as appetising. It's a practice that belongs to all cultures and traditions, particularly those in which food was scarce, where cooking required inventiveness as much as thriftiness.*

With leftovers — meat, rice, polenta, fish and vegetables — Italians often make polpette. *Every region prepares* polpette *differently. In Veneto, these often take the guise of deep-fried rissoles. The classic variants are meat or tuna. Both are served as a cicchetto (the classic Venetian bite-sized snack) with a glass of wine in many of the* bàcari *(wine bars) punctuating the alleys of Venice.*

At Alla Vedova, (a bàcaro *just off the foot-trafficked road connecting the train station to the Rialto Bridge), meat rissoles are produced non-stop. They are eased onto the counter, glowing in their crisp golden glory, and disappear in a matter of seconds. Their fame has built up high expectations, but they manage to exceed them every time. The same can be said for the lovely* polpette di carne *they serve al Al Mercà, just off the Rialto Market: the only issue there is that they are so popular that they sell out too soon.*

I've attempted many meat rissoles variants, but I eventually reverted back to the concept of recupero. *My favourite version now includes a good deal of shredded boiled beef, a bit of* sopressa *to spice things up, and day-old bread — all rolled and fried together into round golden goodness.*

Note: I see this as a winter *cicchetto*, and as such, it's nice paired with a glass of red wine — something spiced but light, to be drunk before a meal, such as Pinot Noir.

Place the potato in a small pan and cover with cold water. Bring to the boil and cook until very tender when pierced with a fork. Drain, peel and mash. Set aside.

In a small bowl, soak the white bread (loosely crumbed) in the milk until softened, about 2 minutes. Squeeze out any excess liquid and transfer the crumbs to a separate, larger bowl. Add the shredded beef, minced *sopressa*, mashed potato and egg. Stir to combine. Now, throw in the garlic and parsley and season. Stir some more, until you have an even mixture. Using your hands, shape the mixture into walnut-sized meatballs and press them down gently to flatten them slightly. Roll them in breadcrumbs and set on a tray or board lined with parchment.

Fill two-thirds of a medium, high-sided frying pan with sunflower oil. Place it over a medium-high heat, and wait until it reaches a temperature of 180°C | 350°F, which you can test with a thermometer or by inserting the handle of a wooden spoon in the oil; when small but fierce bubbles form around the handle, it's ready. Slip a first batch of *polpette* (5–6) into the oil. Fry until lightly browned on both sides, 3–4 minutes each side. Drain and transfer to a large plate covered with kitchen paper. Repeat in batches and serve immediately.

Deep-Fried Cod Rissoles

MAKES 18–20

500g | 1lb 2oz (about 2 large) floury potatoes, peeled and quartered

450g | 1lb salted cod, soaked in cold water for 48 hours (see Note below)

2 bay leaves

2 teaspoons black peppercorns

2 garlic cloves, 1 of them grated

3 eggs, lightly beaten

Finely grated zest of 1 unwaxed lemon

4 tablespoons finely chopped flat-leaf parsley leaves

30g | ¼ cup plain flour

Sunflower oil, for frying

75g | ¾ cup fine dry breadcrumbs

Fine-grain sea salt, to taste

Note: I use salted cod for this recipe — a slightly unorthodox move in Venetian territory, but one that saves some time if you start from scratch. Be aware, though: it still needs to be soaked for 48 hours in cold water, as for stockfish (see page 22).

The hefty dose of lemon and parsley freshens the overall flavour of these polpette (a fish take on the previous recipe), making them a good warm-weather option. I like serving them straight from the frying pan as I pop a bottle of prosecco, or mix a round of spritz (see page 138), either on their own or as part of a cheeky cicchetti feast.

Cook the potatoes in plenty of boiling water until tender, then drain and allow to cool. When they reach room temperature, mash them and season with salt. Set aside.

Drain the cod from its soaking liquid (see Note) and rinse well under running cold water. Place it in a heavy-based pan and cover with more cold water. Add the bay leaves, peppercorns and the 2 whole garlic cloves. Cover with a lid and bring to the boil over a medium heat. As soon as it starts boiling, remove from the heat and let the fish cool in its own cooking water.

Once the cod has cooled a bit — the water should feel neither warm nor cold — drain and transfer to a large bowl, discarding the garlic, bay leaves and peppercorns. Discard the skin and bones and mash the flesh. Add the mashed potatoes, two-thirds of the beaten eggs, grated lemon zest, the grated garlic and the parsley. Stir to combine into a creamy paste. Roll the equivalent of 1 heaped tablespoon of mixture in your hands to form a ball, then press it down to flatten slightly. Gently roll the *polpetta* in flour and then transfer it to a baking tray lined with parchment. Repeat with the remaining mixture.

Fill two-thirds of a medium, high-sided frying pan with sunflower oil. Place it over a medium-high heat, and wait until it reaches a temperature of 180°C | 350°F, which you can test with a thermometer or by inserting the handle of a wooden spoon in the oil (see previous recipe). Dip a first batch of *polpette* (5–6) in the remaining beaten egg, roll them in breadcrumbs, and slip into the oil. Fry until lightly browned on both sides, about 4 minutes each side. Drain and transfer to a large plate covered with kitchen paper. Sprinkle with salt. Repeat in batches and serve as you finish.

Prosciutto & Figs

SERVES 4

16 ripe green or black figs
150g | 5½oz thinly sliced
  prosciutto crudo (such
  as Prosciutto Veneto or
  San Daniele; see page 35)

VARIATION:
Sauté the quartered figs in
a good dose of salted butter
until softened. Drizzle with
1 teaspoon of acacia honey
and serve warm with
prosciutto on toast.

Note: This non-recipe spawns
a lovely, quick starter,
which is at ease alongside
other summery classics like
mozzarella, bean and tomato
salad (see page 212), grilled
vegetables, and green beans
(see page 211).

In late August, the humid heat of the Venetian flatlands tends to subside, giving way to a mild breeze. Meals are still frugal, but regain some substance after days of popsicles and watermelon slices. In the garden, the first of the figs begin to feel tender to the touch. They are gathered in bowls and set on the kitchen table, ready to please those in search of a sugary pick-me-up.

It's the time when figs begin to supplant melon and are paired with prosciutto. I took some convincing at first, mostly because melon and prosciutto are the norm in this part of Italy, and I find it hard to let melon go; but finally I had to surrender to the fact that prosciutto and figs work just as well, and that the patina of salt on the slice of ham seasoning the sugary flesh of the fruit is nothing short of pure alchemy.

Good figs are jammy, supple, a bit squishy, oozing nectar from the base. My favourite are called settembrini; *they are tiny, green and very soft, in season in late August and early September. They are so sweet they make your head spin, and they make a great complement to prosciutto.*

Divide the fig quarters between 4 small plates and ease a few slices of prosciutto onto each. Serve with sliced crusty bread or breadsticks, or both.

Alternatively, set the figs on a large platter and top with prosciutto slices, to which people can help themselves.

Fried Marinated Pumpkin with Onion, Pine Nuts & Raisins

SERVES 4–6

1kg | 2lb 3oz dry-fleshed pumpkin (such as Delica), peeled and deseeded

Sunflower oil, for frying

30ml | 2 tablespoons extra virgin olive oil

500g | 1lb 2oz (about 2 medium) white onions, thinly sliced

60ml | ¼ cup dry white wine

120ml | ½ cup white wine vinegar

40g | ¼ cup raisins, soaked in warm water for 20 minutes

40g | ¼ cup pine nuts, toasted

Fine-grain sea salt and freshly ground black pepper, to taste

I came across this dish in a little trattoria just outside of Venice. It came as part of an antipasti spread and immediately caught my attention. It was a delight: refreshing, with just the right balance of sweetness and astringency.

Raisins and pine nuts convey crunch, chew and a vague aromatic quality to the dish. Traditionally, they were an addition that occured throughout the colder months, when a few extra calories were needed to fight the cold wind blowing across the lagoon.

Slice the pumpkin very finely — about 5mm | ¼ inch thick. The finer you can cut the pumpkin the better. Run a paring knife along the edges of each slice to remove any remaining bits of rind and stringy core. Set aside.

Fill two-thirds of a medium, high-sided frying pan with sunflower oil. Place it over a medium-high heat, and wait until it reaches a temperature of 180°C | 350°F, which you can test with a thermometer or by inserting the handle of a wooden spoon in the oil; when small but fierce bubbles form around the handle, it's ready. Now, slip in a first batch of pumpkin slices, trying not to crowd them. Fry for 2–3 minutes each side, or until their edges appear crisp. Drain with a slotted spoon and transfer to a plate covered with kitchen paper. Continue frying until you've finished all the slices. Sprinkle with a little salt and set aside.

To make the marinade (*saor*), heat the olive oil in a separate frying pan. Add the sliced onions and fry gently over a medium-low heat until they appear very soft but not browned, stirring often. Pour in the wine and vinegar and season with salt and pepper. Increase the heat to medium-high and let it evaporate for a couple of minutes.

In a glass bowl, arrange a layer of pumpkin. Cover with a layer of white onions and sprinkle with a few raisins (drained) and pine nuts. Repeat in layers until you have finished all the ingredients. Pour over any remaining cooking liquid, which will act as a marinade. Leave to cool to room temperature, then wrap with cling film and place in the fridge to marinate for 24 hours, or up to 2 days. Serve at room temperature.

Scallop Gratin with Almonds & Orange

SERVES 4

12 king scallops in half shell
(see Note below)

45ml | 3 tablespoons extra
virgin olive oil

1 garlic clove, whole but
lightly crushed

Finely grated zest and juice
of 1 unwaxed orange

100g | 1 cup ground almonds

100g | 1 cup fine dry
breadcrumbs

Fine-grain sea salt, to taste

I have a deep fondness for capesante gratinate. They set the tone of a meal (refined but not stuffy), and suggest that more seafood will follow, which is always good news. In Venice, the gratin part doesn't involve any béchamel or cream. Rather, the flavour of the fish sings solo, with fresh secondary notes — parsley, wine, oil (sometimes butter), garlic and citrus. Breadcrumbs are often called for, as they crisp up under the heat of the grill, creating a lovely contrast to the soft mollusc.

As an alternative to the usual Venetian flavours, I have found the combination of orange zest and almond works blissfully with baked scallops. This is particularly true when oranges come into season in early winter (which happens to be a good time for scallops as well) and the essential oils contained in their skin are at their strongest.

Note: Opt for scallops with the orange part (coral), which is a delicacy and adds flavour.

Preheat the oven to 200°C | 400°F | gas mark 6. Remove the scallops from their shell and scrub the shell clean. Wash the scallops under cold running water and pat them dry. Set aside.

In a medium bowl, make a marinade with the oil, garlic and the orange juice, strained, and salt, to taste. Gently toss the scallops in it and leave them to marinate for 10 minutes. Meanwhile, in a separate bowl combine the ground almonds with the breadcrumbs and the grated orange zest.

Line a baking tray with parchment and arrange the scallop shells on top. In each, pour in a little of the marinade liquid and then ease the scallops on top. Cover with a bit of the almond mixture and sprinkle with a pinch of salt.

Bake for 10 minutes. Preheat the grill (or turn on the grill function) and crisp up for 3 more minutes, or until deeply golden on the surface. Transfer to a platter or individual plates, and serve right away.

CAPELONGHE CON AGLIO E PREZZEMOLO
Razor Clams with Garlic & Parsley

SERVES 4

1kg | 2lb 3oz razor clams,
  soaked in salted water
  (see Note below)
80ml | ⅓ cup dry white wine
30ml | 2 tablespoons extra
  virgin olive oil
Juice of ½ lemon
2 garlic cloves, very finely
  chopped
2 tablespoons finely chopped
  flat-leaf parsley leaves
Fine-grain sea salt and freshly
  ground black pepper, to taste

Note: Avoid buying razor
clams in the summer, as it's
not their season. Ensure that
they are alive (touch them
gently; they should move),
and that their shells are intact.
Try to cook them the same
day you buy them, too. Razor
clams live in sandy sea beds,
so they are best soaked in
salted water (as salty as the
sea) for about 2 hours prior to
cooking, in order to disgorge
any grains of sand.

Capelonghe *(literally 'long shells') is the Venetian name for* cannolicchi, *razor clams. Locals don't even bother calling them with the Italian name; the dialectal form is far more intuitive. Along the Venetian lagoon,* capelonghe *are often included in seafood platters served as antipasto, usually steamed and seasoned with oil, parsley and garlic (or onion).*

Unlike scallops (see page 153), with which I like to experiment using different flavour combinations, with capelonghe *I don't dare go off the beaten track. When perfectly fresh, their sweetness is so striking, so very moving, that my culinary adventurousness fades; I become a creature of habit. And so, here is a classic recipe. It's a good example of* la cucina degli ingredienti, *a style of cooking that is vital to Veneto and that prioritises good ingredients over fussy preparations.*

Wash the clams thoroughly under cold running water. Place a large frying pan over a high heat. Once hot, add the clams and wine. Cover with a tight-fitting lid and steam just until the clams have opened, about 2 minutes.

Transfer the clams to a plate. Using a pair of scissors, remove the siphon, the foot and the stomach (basically any dark meat). Put the white meat back in the shells and keep warm.

Strain the cooking juices left in the frying pan and whisk them with the oil and lemon juice. Reduce the volume of the liquid by simmering it over a gentle heat for 5 minutes; then stir in the garlic, parsley and salt and pepper to taste. Drizzle the dressing over the razor clams and serve.

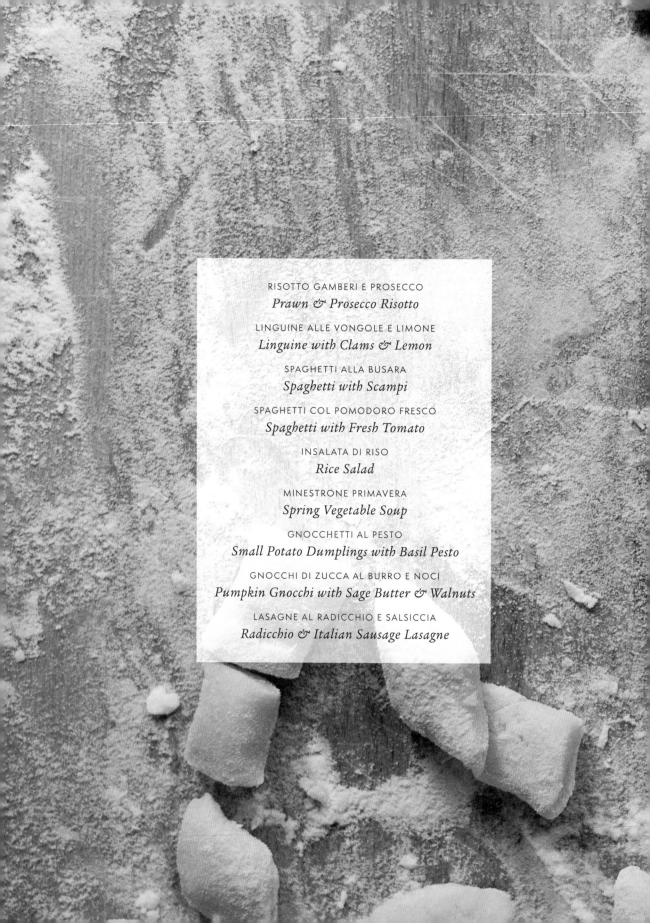

RISOTTO GAMBERI E PROSECCO
Prawn & Prosecco Risotto

LINGUINE ALLE VONGOLE E LIMONE
Linguine with Clams & Lemon

SPAGHETTI ALLA BUSARA
Spaghetti with Scampi

SPAGHETTI COL POMODORO FRESCO
Spaghetti with Fresh Tomato

INSALATA DI RISO
Rice Salad

MINESTRONE PRIMAVERA
Spring Vegetable Soup

GNOCCHETTI AL PESTO
Small Potato Dumplings with Basil Pesto

GNOCCHI DI ZUCCA AL BURRO E NOCI
Pumpkin Gnocchi with Sage Butter & Walnuts

LASAGNE AL RADICCHIO E SALSICCIA
Radicchio & Italian Sausage Lasagne

PRIMI

Prawn & Prosecco Risotto

SERVES 4

1kg | 2lb 3oz king prawns,
  shelled and cleaned (heads
  and carcasses reserved)
75g | ⅓ cup unsalted butter
1 golden onion, finely chopped
360g | heaped 1¾ cups
  risotto rice (Carnaroli or
  Vialone Nano)
240ml | 1 cup prosecco,
  ideally Prosecco DOCG
Fine-grain sea salt and freshly
  ground black pepper, to taste

This is the story of how this risotto came to be — quite by chance — and of how it became one of my favourite seafood dishes of all time.

One Sunday, at around noon, my husband and I had opened a bottle of nice prosecco to kick start a leisurely weekend lunch. Having purchased a bundle of prawns from the market that same morning, we settled on a pot of prawn risotto. Soon after I started cooking, I realised that I had run out of my 'usual' deglazing wine. 'Use some of this' he said, gesturing at the open bottle on the table. Nonsense, I thought. What a waste! But the rice was already hissing, so I reluctantly grabbed the prosecco and poured a generous splash into the pot, which began to seethe furiously, as if to say: about time. Sweet vapours swirled up, and somehow, in the haze of the moment, I saw that it was the start of something good.

The risotto was a surprise. The higher sugar content in the prosecco backed up the sweetness of the prawns, creating a special bond between the two (the generous knob of butter I added at the end also helped, no doubt). The wine left in the bottle, drunk with abandon, cleansed the palate and cut through the creaminess, leaving one wishing for more of everything. To which I would say: be generous with portions (those I listed below most definitely are), as second helpings will inevitably happen.

Store the shelled prawns in the fridge while you prepare the fumet. Place the prawn heads and carcasses in a large pan and cover with 2 litres | 8⅓ cups of water. Place over a medium heat and cook for 30 minutes from when the water reaches the boil, stirring and squeezing the heads with a wooden spoon so that they release their juices. Strain the liquid and place back in the pan. Set it over a low heat and keep it warm.

Next, melt 30g | 2 tablespoons of the butter in a large heavy-based frying pan set over a medium-high heat. When hot and bubbly, add the shelled prawns. Sauté for about 2 minutes, season with salt and pepper and then remove from the heat and set aside.

CONTINUED OVERLEAF

Set a separate heavy-based pan over a medium heat. Fry the onion in half the remaining butter and, once soft, add the rice. Toast it for a couple of minutes, stirring very frequently so that it doesn't stick to the bottom. When the rice is opaque and hissing, pour in the prosecco. Allow it to reduce, stirring all the while, and then start adding the hot prawn stock, 1–2 ladlefuls at a time, adding more as soon as it's absorbed. Carry on this way until the rice is tender but still al dente, about 15 minutes. A couple of minutes before removing the rice from the heat, stir in the prawns. Taste and adjust the seasoning; add a last splash of stock if the risotto appears too dense.

Once done, turn off the heat and add the remaining butter. 'Whip' and stir the risotto energetically for a couple of minutes (this will make it creamier and lighter), then serve immediately.

Linguine with Clams & Lemon

SERVES 4

1kg | 2lb 3oz fresh clams in
the shell, soaked in salted
water (see Note below)
60ml | ¼ cup extra virgin
olive oil
3 garlic cloves, whole but
lightly crushed
120ml | ½ cup dry white wine
400g | 14oz linguine
4 tablespoons finely chopped
flat-leaf parsley leaves
Finely grated zest of
1 unwaxed lemon
Fine-grain sea salt and freshly
ground black pepper, to taste

Note: Make sure that the
clams have closed, undamaged
shells, or else discard them.
Soak them in salted water
(as salty as the sea) for at least
2 hours prior to cooking to
give them time to disgorge
their sand.

In Veneto, pasta coi caparossoli — using the sort of fat, ridged clams native to the area — is a classic along the coast. For mollusc lovers like myself, it's also a frequent craving, so whenever I find fresh clams at the market I feast on them like it was my last meal, often with a glass of the same wine I used to daze the bivalves.

Perhaps because it's a dish that occurs often in my kitchen, I find myself wanting to twist the basic pasta con le vongole recipe by adding a wild card: monk's beard (agretti) is a favourite for its tang and colour; but also, quite simply, lots of lemon zest, a powerhouse of aroma and freshness able to brighten up any seafood dish with a surge of Mediterranean flavours.

Drain the clams and rinse well until you can't see any trace of sand or debris. Heat 2 tablespoons of the oil and 1 garlic clove in a large frying pan over a medium-high heat. When hot, add the clams and pour in the wine. Cover and shake so that the clams spread evenly. Cook until they are all open, about 5 minutes.

Remove the clams from the pan and transfer them to a plate; remove three-quarters of them from their shells and discard any that didn't open. Strain and reserve the liquid left in the frying pan to remove any grit or little stones, as well as the garlic.

Bring a large pan of salted water to the boil. When it reaches a rolling boil, add the linguine. Meanwhile, set the same large frying pan in which you opened the clams over a medium heat. Add the remaining oil and garlic cloves and fry until fragrant. Discard the garlic and pour in the clam liquid. Taste and adjust the seasoning.

When the pasta is al dente, drain it and add it to the frying pan to finish cooking it in the clam liquid. Toss it continuously so that it absorbs the liquid. At the very end, add the reserved shelled clams and sauté with the linguine for 30 seconds. Finally, add the remaining clams still in their shell, sprinkle with parsley and top with lemon zest. Finish with freshly ground black pepper, toss once more and serve.

Spaghetti with Scampi

SERVES 4

1kg | 2lb 3oz scampi

60ml | ¼ cup extra virgin
olive oil

1 golden onion, finely chopped

2 garlic cloves, whole but
lightly crushed

2 dried chillies (or ¼ teaspoon
chilli flakes)

180ml | ¾ cup dry white wine

700g | 1½lb (about 5-6) fresh
plum tomatoes, peeled (see
Note opposite), deseeded
and chopped (or use 700g |
1½lb fresh cherry tomatoes,
finely chopped)

400g | 14oz spaghetti

1 tablespoon very finely
chopped flat-leaf
parsley leaves

Fine-grain sea salt and freshly
ground black pepper, to taste

Every year in July the charming maritime city of Chioggia (often referred to as 'la piccola Venezia', The Little Venice) hosts a big festival, the sagra del pesce, *celebrating its long-held fishing tradition and wonderful seafood cuisine. It has recently become an unmissable event for my parents — a sort of new family tradition, which I am happy to honour whenever I happen to be around (you'll never see me bailing out from the prospect of a seafood feast).*

Along the main pedestrian street, arrays of stalls offer a series of seafood-based piatti tipici *at reasonable prices: from* fritto misto *(see page 85) to* risotto di pesce, *from* peoci in cassopipa *(steamed mussels in parsley sauce) to* baccalà *(see pages 21–22). The dynamics — well — those resemble any other food festival in Italy. Patrons form scattered queues in front of the cashier, yell their order to the overwhelmed lady at the till, wait (impatiently) for a table to clear, sit down — not without pestering the tables nearby, finish a first jug of prosecco (rigorously on tap), go for a second round (hear their name, pick up their order), sit down bothering everybody once more, and finally tuck in with gusto, leaving behind a trail of emptied bivalve shells. It's a fun, folkloristic experience; a full immersion in the atmosphere of the place, and an occasion to eat some very delicious fish.*

It was at this sagra del pesce *that I first tasted* spaghetti alla busara. *I had never come across it before (a sign of how many facets regional Italian cuisine can have, and of how different food can be even between two neighbouring towns); I was intrigued. Needless to say, I was pretty pleased to see some fat scampi coming my way as my order reached the table. The sauce itself turned out to be of the simplest kind (just tomato, parsley and a hint of chilli, all brought together by olive oil and wine) but impeccable in its basic nature; no need to mess about with good scampi after all.*

Since then, spaghetti alla busara *has become the sort of pasta I like making for friends when cooking Venetian. It's impressive and yet unfussy, refined but a bit messy, and it asks for licking your fingers like there's no tomorrow. I like to think of it as a feast in itself.*

Notes: The Adriatic is renowned for its shellfish, which is why they are heavily featured in Venetian cuisine. Having said that, use whatever delicious crustacean is caught near you (prawns work well, too). When seafood is involved, freshness and proximity are far more important than precisely following a recipe.

To peel tomatoes, score their skin crossways, place in a bowl and pour over boiling water. Wait 30 seconds. Drain and plunge in cold water. The skin should slip off easily at this point.

Start by cleaning the scampi. Wash them thoroughly under cold running water, then slit the back and remove the black thread (intestine). Set aside.

Heat the oil in a large frying pan and fry the onion over a medium heat until soft and translucent. Add the garlic and the chillies and stir. Let them infuse the oil for a couple of minutes (reduce the heat if they look like burning), then throw in the scampi and increase the heat to high. Season with salt and pepper and sauté for 2 minutes, then remove from the pan and set aside. Pour in the wine; allow it to reduce over a very high heat and then add the chopped tomatoes. Reduce the heat to medium, cover and cook for 15–20 minutes, until the tomatoes appear saucy. If during this time the sauce dries out excessively, add a drop of water. Turn off the heat and cover to keep warm.

Bring a large pan of salted water to the boil. Cook the spaghetti very al dente — about 3 minutes short of the suggested cooking time — reserving about 250ml | 1 cup of cooking water. Drain and transfer to the pan with the tomato sauce and add the scampi, too. Place over a medium-high heat and pour in the reserved cooking water. Toss until the pasta has absorbed most of the liquid and is nicely coated in sauce. Sprinkle with parsley and toss some more to combine. Serve right away.

Spaghetti with Fresh Tomato

SERVES 4

1kg | 2lb 3oz ripe San
  Marzano tomatoes, peeled
  (see Note on page 165),
  deseeded and finely chopped
6 garlic cloves, thinly sliced
10–12 basil leaves,
  roughly torn
400g | 14oz spaghetti
45ml | 3 tablespoons extra
  virgin olive oil
Fine-grain sea salt and freshly
  ground black pepper, to taste

Note: The flavours here are
very basic, but quite special in
their own right, so it's more
important than ever to use
ripe, flavoursome tomatoes,
and the best oil you can lay
your hands on. Finish your
pasta with grated Parmesan
if you like; I usually leave it
out to let the tomatoes shine
through.

With both sets of grandparents growing a good amount of prolific tomato plants in their gardens, we would sometimes find ourselves struggling to consume all their fruits. The foremost plan was to feast on tomatoes until we could eat no more, and to make sauce (see pages 256–257) with whatever was left.

Mum enjoyed turning the soft San Marzano tomatoes left on the bottom of the crate into what she used to call sugo di pomodoro fresco. *It is nothing more than an uncooked sauce made with chopped tomatoes infused with lots of new season garlic, basil for brightness and freshness, and some good olive oil to bring it all together. The sauce, stirred quickly into pasta with some of its starchy water, produces the perfect seasonal spaghetti bowl — hot, yet still suitable for a humid Venetian summer night.*

Place the chopped tomatoes, garlic and basil in a colander set over a bowl. Season with salt and pepper; toss to combine. Cover with a plate and leave to macerate for about 1 hour.

Next, bring a large pan of salted water to a rolling boil. Add the spaghetti and cook very al dente — about 3 minutes short of the suggested cooking time. When the pasta is about ready, place a large frying pan over a high heat and keep it ready. Drain the pasta and transfer it to the pan together with the tomato mixture in the colander and the olive oil.

Finish cooking the pasta with the sauce, adding a good splash of the liquid in the bowl released by the tomatoes to help it come together. Keep cooking the pasta for 2–3 minutes, tossing and turning so that it absorbs the liquid. The sauce should eventually look like an emulsion of sorts, with the tomato chunks softened. At this point, it's ready to serve.

INSALATA DI RISO
Rice Salad

SERVES 6–8

500g | 2½ cups risotto rice
(such as Vialone Nano
or Carnaroli)

4 eggs

750g | 1lb 10oz *giardiniera*
(see page 260), or mixed
pickled/preserved vegetables
(baby onions, cornichons,
peppers etc.), diced

100g | 3½oz artichokes in oil,
drained and chopped

100g | 3½oz pitted green
olives, sliced

100g | 3½oz pitted black
or kalamata olives, sliced

30g | 1oz capers, rinsed

200g | 7oz tuna in extra
virgin olive oil (drained
weight), flaked

150g | 5¼oz aged cheese
(such as Asiago or
Piave), diced

2 tablespoons finely chopped
flat-leaf parsley leaves
(optional)

Fine-grain sea salt, to taste

Some think of insalata di riso *as the joke food of the 1990s — a garish medley of dubious nature to be eaten under tacky colourful umbrellas on very tacky beaches. I dare to disagree. Maybe I am so nostalgically attached to* insalata di riso *that my judgement is biased, but I still think it's a brilliant invention, whose popularity shouldn't be ignored. After all, summer days on the humid, mosquito-infested coasts of Veneto wouldn't be the same without it.*

The concept is simple: white rice stirred with whatever strikes your fancy — sundried tomatoes, capers, tomatoes, tuna, ham, cheese, salami, eggs, olives, pickles... Of course, the better the ingredients, the tastier your salad will be, and quality is the key to the success of this dish.

Classic combinations include giardiniera *(see page 260), cubed ham, cubed hard cheese, hard-boiled eggs, olives and tinned tuna. I've suggested a favourite mix below; feel free to ignore it and make up your own medley, then pack it in plastic containers and take it to the beach or to the park, for there's no better place to enjoy* insalata di riso *than outdoors.*

———————

Bring a large pan of water to the boil. Add the rice and a generous dash of salt and cook for 15 minutes, or until tender but still al dente. Drain and rinse under cold running water to eliminate the starch and cool it off. Leave in the colander to drain properly while you take care of the rest.

Place the eggs in a small pan and bring to the boil. As soon as the water starts boiling, remove from the heat and cover the pan. Leave for 10 minutes, then drain and cool under cold running water. Peel the eggs and set aside.

In a large bowl, combine the giardiniera or chopped pickles, artichokes, olives, capers, tuna and cheese. Add the rice, too, and stir to combine. Finally, add the parsley and toss to incorporate. Taste and adjust the seasoning if needed. Quarter the eggs and arrange them on top.

Chill the rice salad for at least 1 hour before serving.

Spring Vegetable Soup

SERVES 4

30ml | 2 tablespoons extra
  virgin olive oil
½ golden onion, finely
  chopped
1 small carrot, peeled
  and finely diced
1 celery stick, trimmed
  and finely chopped
200g | 7oz green beans,
  trimmed and chopped
200g | 7oz shelled broad
  beans
250g | 2 cups shelled peas
150g | 5oz green asparagus,
  trimmed and sliced into
  5mm- | ¼-inch-long pieces
1 litre | 4¼ cups vegetable
  stock, heated
130g | 4½oz tubetti or
  ditalini pasta
2 tablespoons very finely
  chopped flat-leaf
  parsley leaves
Fine-grain sea salt, to taste
4 sprigs of thyme, to garnish
  (optional)

As a lover of soup, I tend to eat it no matter what time of year (a habit that I inherited from Mum's weekly minestrone, see page 44). The ingredients list changes to mirror the seasons, and the serving temperature might vary depending on the weather, but the frequency with which it appears on our table remains largely unchanged.

The idea for this springy soup sparked from a variety of sources, but was partly inspired by the famous risotto primavera *served at Locanda Cipriani, on the Venetian island of Torcello — a dish made with the most tender, verdant spring vegetables. Not unlike Cipriani's risotto, every ingredient in this soup is distinguishable, every flavour clean and crisp, delicate yet defined. Its glorious greenness decrees the end of winter and a change of mood in the kitchen, and yet, you'll find that its nourishing, warming nature will go hand in hand with those still-not-so-warm early spring days.*

Heat the oil in a large pan over a medium heat. Add the onion, carrot and celery and fry gently, moving it every now and then, until the onion is soft and translucent and the carrot and celery are tender. Add the green beans first, and cook for a couple of minutes, stirring to coat in oil; then add the broad beans, peas and asparagus (except for the tips, which should be reserved for the end). Fry everything for 5 minutes or so, until glistening with oil and tender but not mushy.

At this point, pour in the warm stock and bring to a simmer. Taste and adjust the seasoning, then add the pasta. Cook it until al dente, stirring frequently. At the very end, stir in the parsley and asparagus tips and cook for 1 more minute.

Transfer to warm bowls and garnish with a sprig of thyme.

Small Potato Dumplings with Basil Pesto

SERVES 4

For the gnocchetti:

1kg | 2lb 3oz waxy potatoes
(roughly the same size)

200–250g | 1⅔–2 cups plain
flour, plus more as needed

1 teaspoon fine-grain sea salt

1 egg (optional)

For the basil pesto:

85g | 3oz basil leaves

20g | ¾oz Parmesan,
crumbled

½ small garlic clove
(about 2g), inner shoot
removed, sliced

15g | 1½ tablespoons
pine nuts

¼ teaspoon fine-grain sea salt

120ml | ½ cup extra virgin
olive oil, plus more for
covering the pesto

Following Mum's example, I have long been reluctant to make potato gnocchi from scratch — too risky, too messy. I eventually gathered the courage to give it a go and discovered that yes, they are a bit laborious, but the result more than justifies the effort. The difference between commercial and home-made gnocchi is substantial: when done well, these are so airy and light that they basically melt in your mouth. No packaged gnocchi will ever give you that thrill.

What I learnt in my relatively short but dedicated gnocchi-making experience is to beware of flour. When used in excess, flour leads to chewy gnocchi, which is easily the worst thing that can happen to them — other than falling apart in boiling water. The amount of flour needed to bring the dough together varies depending on the type of potatoes used (waxy versus floury) and the way they are cooked (boiled versus baked). Opinions differ greatly here, but in my experience, I found that waxy potatoes produce lighter gnocchi.

As for the way to cook them, I switch between boiling and roasting depending on the mood. Roasting your spuds produces fluffy potato flakes that need very little flour to come together. However, boiling the potatoes whole, skin on, and then drying them in a hot frying pan produces flakes that are just as light. What counts in the end is the feel of the dough: small variations are inevitable and need to be embraced rather than dreaded. Practice is the only way to gain confidence and produce impeccable gnocchi at every attempt.

Gnocchetti are the small, grooveless version of gnocchi. Venetians are very fond of them and like tossing them with seafood sauces. Personally, I like them with a generous dollop of basil pesto. It's a habit I inherited from Mum, whose pesto has always been spectacular, especially when made with Grandpa's violently perfumed basil. And so, nostalgically, pesto is the way I season gnocchetti whenever summer and good basil are in full swing.

CONTINUED OVERLEAF

For the pesto, place all the ingredients except for the oil in the container of a hand-held stick blender. Pour in half the oil and start pulsing in short, regular intervals to break down the ingredients. Slowly pour in the rest of the oil and carry on blending until you have a smooth, creamy, slightly loose pesto. Add a little more oil to cover the surface and then cover the glass with its lid or a piece of foil and set it in the fridge until ready to use.

Next, preheat the oven to 190°C | 375°F | gas mark 5. Brush the potatoes with cool water, pat them dry, prick them all over with a fork and arrange on a baking tray lined with parchment. Bake for about 1 hour or until cooked all the way through. Remove from the oven and allow them to cool to a manageable temperature before peeling them. Alternatively, boil the potatoes whole, skin on, until cooked through, and then transfer them to a hot frying pan until dry on all sides. Allow them to cool and then peel them.

Scatter three-quarters of the flour mixed with the salt over a work surface. Press the potato flesh through a ricer or a fine sieve onto the flour; add the egg now, if using. Shape everything into a soft ball of dough — add the rest of the flour, a little at the time, until you reach the right texture (pliable and soft, but not sticky). Dust the work surface with more flour and divide the dough into 4–5 chunks. Using your palms and working from the centre, roll out the dough into long ropes that are as thick as your ring finger. Cut each rope into square segments and transfer them to a flour-dusted tray or board.

Bring a large pan of water to a rolling boil. Salt it, and when boiling again, tip in about half the *gnocchetti* (I usually cook these in 2 batches).

Stir and wait for them to float before draining them with a slotted spoon and transferring them to a warm platter. Repeat with the rest, then season with the pesto and serve immediately.

Pumpkin Gnocchi with Sage Butter & Walnuts

SERVES 4

For the gnocchi:
1kg | 2lb 3oz dry-fleshed
   pumpkin, skin on (see
   Note below)
1 teaspoon fine-grain sea salt
1 egg
200–300g | 1⅓–2 cups plain
   flour, sifted
Freshly ground nutmeg

For the sauce:
90g | 6 tablespoons
   unsalted butter
5 large sage leaves
Freshly ground black pepper
   (optional)
50g | 1½oz Grana Padano,
   grated
50g | 1½oz walnuts,
   roughly chopped

Note: Using a dry-fleshed
pumpkin here is very
important. The drier the flesh,
the lower the amount of flour
required and the better the
final result. Top pumpkin
types for the task are Delica
or Kabocha, but Crown
Prince can work, too. As for
the disputable use of eggs
in gnocchi, I always add one
when making these, as they'll
be too fragile otherwise.

Making gnocchi using the tawny flesh of a sweet pumpkin has been part of the Venetian culinary heritage for centuries. Veneto is indeed a land where pumpkins and squashes grow bountifully, developing a sweet and nicely firm flesh. They are usually harvested in late summer, then stored in a dry place and eaten in all manners (see, Risi e Suca and Zucca in Saor, pages 56 and 150), including in the shape of gnocchi.

The classic sauce for pumpkin gnocchi, traditionally made for Saint Michael's Day on 29 September, is cinnamon, sugar, butter and cheese. For my part, I prefer keeping things on the savoury side by seasoning mine with a buttery sauce infused with a handful of musty sage leaves, a sprinkle of chopped walnuts, and a generous snowfall of grated Grana.

Pumpkin-based gnocchi can be made two ways: either by rolling the dough in thin ropes and cutting out little knots, similarly to potato gnocchi (see previous page); or by tipping small amounts of dough straight into a pot of rolling-boil water using two spoons. This last method produces the sort of feathery knots I like, and it's the one I'm sharing here.

Preheat the oven to 200°C | 400°F | gas mark 6.

Scrape the seeds and strings from the centre of the pumpkin, then cut it into 2–3 slices of the same size and ease them onto a baking sheet lined with parchment. Roast for about 1 hour, or until very soft, turning the slices half way through the cooking time. Remove from the oven and allow to cool to room temperature.

Scrape the pumpkin flesh off the skin and transfer it to a sieve or chinois. Leave it to let off as much water as possible, moving the pulp every now and then to facilitate the process. This should take 4–6 hours, depending on the type of pumpkin. Aim for less than half the initial weight — about 420–450g | 15oz of drained purée.

CONTINUED OVERLEAF

VARIATION:

On occasion, I toss these with a big spoonful of *gorgonzola dolce* melted in a tiny bit of milk. If you like blue cheese, I encourage you to give it a try: it's a real treat.

Place the drained pumpkin, salt and egg in a large bowl, and stir to combine. Start adding the flour in small increments, working your dough with a spoon to incorporate it before adding more. You might need a little less or a little more depending on how wet your pumpkin purée is, but aim for a fairly creamy texture that you can scoop and shape easily.

Bring a large pan of salted water to the boil. Using 2 teaspoons, shape a grape-size dollop of dough and ease it into the boiling water. Repeat with the rest of the dough (dip your spoons in the boiling water in between scoops to help the gnocchi slide off), draining the gnocchi when they float and transferring them onto a warm serving plate.

For the sauce, melt the butter in a large frying pan over a medium heat. Add the sage and fry for a couple of minutes, until fragrant. When ready, add the gnocchi and sauté them for 1 minute, just enough for them to be nicely coated in the butter sauce.

Remove from the heat and season with a generous dusting of freshly ground nutmeg and a bit of black pepper, if liked. Serve the gnocchi with grated Grana and a small handful of chopped walnuts.

Radicchio & Italian Sausage Lasagne

SERVES 6

For the béchamel sauce:

1 litre | 4¼ cups whole milk

75g | ⅓ cup unsalted butter

80g | ⅔ cup plain flour, sifted

Freshly grated nutmeg

Fine-grain sea salt, to taste

For the radicchio layer:

700g | 1½lb (about 3 large
  heads) radicchio tardivo
  (see Note right)

30g | 2 tablespoons
  unsalted butter

½ golden onion, finely
  chopped

80ml | ⅓ cup dry white wine

Fine-grain sea salt and freshly
  ground black pepper, to taste

For the sausage layer:

200g | 7oz *luganega* or other
  Italian pork sausage

250–300g | 8¾oz–10½oz
  fresh pasta sheets (see
  Note right)

100g | 3½oz Grana Padano,
  grated

Radicchio tardivo grown in the Treviso province is the most prized among all chicories. Tardivo is a forced variety, meaning that it requires a very specific type of climate and lots of care to develop into the bittersweet, crimson and white curly beauty it is.

In season from late autumn to the end of winter, good tardivo is a marvellously refreshing leaf — crisp, sprightly and snappy, with a flavour that is far more delicate than other radicchio varieties. All these unique features, of course, make it a very sought-after type, impacting its availability and price. Even in Veneto, tardivo is often reserved for special occasions.

This lasagne fits the special occasion requirement just fine. Here, tucked between thin layers of pasta sheets and voluptuous dollops of béchamel, tardivo is at home; its vague bitter accent is slightly subdued by the sweetness of the sauce and the savouriness of the sausage, but not to the point of being overshadowed; the flavours are in balance, and radicchio remains the undisputed star of the dish.

———————

For the béchamel sauce, heat the milk in a small pan until it's about to reach the boil. Remove it from the heat and keep it warm. In a separate, heavy-based pan, melt the butter over a medium-low heat. When it starts to foam, stir in the flour and whisk until combined into a paste. Remove the pan from the heat momentarily and pour over the milk in a thin stream, whisking all the while. Place the pan back on the hob and cook the sauce until you see it starting to thicken, about 5 minutes. Season with salt and freshly grated nutmeg; stir, cover and set aside.

Wash the radicchio and pat it dry. Trim the roots and cut the heads into thin strips. Next, heat the butter in a large frying pan over a medium heat. Add the onion and cook it, stirring often, until soft and translucent, about 5 minutes. Add the shredded radicchio and cook for about 5 minutes, until wilted. Then, pour in the wine and allow it to evaporate; season, cover and carry on cooking for a further 10 minutes, until the radicchio is very soft. Remove from the heat and set aside.

Notes: If you can't source tardivo, the long and slim trevisano is a good alternative. The round chioggiotto will do the trick, too, but it won't perform as well as the others. As for the sausage, in Veneto we are partial to luganega — a long, thin, cord-like pork sausage made with cheek and neck meat. A classic Italian sausage is also good, as long as it doesn't contain fennel seeds.

To make lasagne sheets, follow the same procedure described in the Note on page 62, but cut the dough into large rectangles instead of thin tagliatelle. If you are using your own fresh pasta, par-boil the sheets prior to layering. If, on the other hand, you are using store-bought pasta sheets, check the packet for instructions: most brands of pasta don't need to be par-boiled.

To cook the sausage, discard the casing and crumble the meat in a hot dry frying pan set over a medium-high heat. Pan-fry until browned and cooked through, about 5 minutes. Set aside.

Finally, par-boil the fresh pasta sheets (see Note left). Working in batches, cook the sheets for 2 minutes in plenty of boiling salted water. Drain them with a slotted spoon and plunge them in a bowl filled with cold water. Leave them there for 1 minute, then drain them again and lay them in a single layer on clean tea towels to dry.

When ready to assemble the lasagne, preheat the oven to 200°C | 390°F | gas mark 6. Smear the bottom of a baking dish (about 35 × 25 × 7cm | 14 × 10 × 3 inches) with a couple of spoonfuls of béchamel. Next, arrange a layer of pasta sheets, trying not to overlap them too much (trim any extras). Add a couple of spoonfuls of béchamel to cover, scatter some radicchio and sausage on top and then sprinkle with grated Grana. Repeat 3 more times (so as to have 4 layers in total), trying to end with a layer of radicchio covered by a few splashes of béchamel and any leftover Grana.

Cover with foil and place in the middle shelf of the oven, Bake for 25–30 minutes, or until golden and bubbly on top. Uncover it and finish cooking it under a hot grill for about 3–4 minutes, so that the surface can turn crispy. Allow to rest for 10–15 minutes before serving.

SGOMBRO AGLI ODORI
Poached Mackerel with Aromatics

ORATA AL FORNO CON LE PATATE
Baked Gilthead Bream with Potatoes

BRANZINO AL CARTOCCIO
Sea Bass Parcels

FOLPETTI E PATATE
Baby Octopus & Potato Salad

CALAMARI RIPIENI
Stuffed Squid

SPEZZATINO
Slow-Cooked Beef Stew

BOLLITO DI MANZO E SALSA VERDE
Beef Pot Roast with Parsley Sauce

GALLINA UBRIACA
Hen in Red Wine

POLPETTE AL SUGO
Meatballs in Tomato Sauce

SECONDI

Poached Mackerel with Aromatics

SERVES 4

1 carrot, peeled and halved
lengthways

1 golden onion, quartered

2 garlic cloves

2 celery sticks

Small bunch of flat-leaf
parsley

2 teaspoons peppercorns

2 bay leaves

4 whole mackerel (about 300g
| 10½oz each), cleaned

Juice of ½ lemon

30ml | 2 tablespoons extra
virgin olive oil

Fine-grain sea salt, to taste

Note: Cooked this way,
mackerel is excellent served
hot, but also at room
temperature, particularly
in the summer. Pair it with
some lemony (preferably
home-made) mayonnaise
if you like the idea.

Mackerel has a strong flavour that splits opinion, but it also has a lot going on for it: it is sustainable and widely available, in Italy and elsewhere; it has a long series of health benefits; and most of all, it can be prepared in many ways. Boiled might seem like the least exciting of them, but it just works, even more so with the support of the magic mix called odori: *celery, carrot, onion, sometimes parsley and garlic. Odori (aromatics) are the pillars of Italian cuisine, and of* cucina povera *in particular. Finely chopped in a* battuto, *they add character to the most simple soup, sauce or stew; whole, they impart flavour to stock as much as to a boiling piece of meat (as in the* bollito *on page 198) or, in this case, fish.*

Here, the odori *are split into two teams: carrot, onion and celery are added to the cooking liquid to mitigate the sharpness of the fish, while finely chopped garlic and parsley are paired with delicate, fruity olive oil and zingy lemon juice in a dressing that elevates this humble dish to a triumph of flavours.*

Place the carrot, onion, 1 garlic clove, celery, half the parsley, the peppercorns, bay leaves and a pinch of salt in a rectangular pan big enough to host the fish. Fill three-quarters of it with cold water. Place it over a very low heat and let the liquid reduce for 30 minutes.

Next, add the fish, ensuring that it's completely submerged in the liquid (top it up, if needed). Simmer for 15 minutes over a very low heat. Drain the mackerel and discard the *odori*. Meanwhile, pick the leaves from the remaining parsley and chop it very finely with the remaining garlic clove.

Open the fish and remove the spine and as many bones as possible. Ease the fish fillets onto a serving platter, skin-side down. Season with the lemon juice, olive oil, salt, and the finely chopped parsley and garlic.

Baked Gilthead Bream with Potatoes

SERVES 4

45ml | 3 tablespoons extra
  virgin olive oil
800g | 1lb 12oz (about
  5 medium) waxy potatoes,
  peeled
2 medium sea bream
  (about 600g | 1lb 5oz each),
  cleaned (see Notes below)
60ml | ¼ cup dry white wine
Fine-grain sea salt and freshly
  ground black pepper, to taste
1 unwaxed lemon, to serve

Notes: Of all the types of
bream to be found at the
market, wild-caught gilthead
bream is, I believe, the tastiest.
Late spring and summer are
when to make the most of
it, though sea bass can be
substituted just fine. Ask your
fishmonger for guidance.

When baking whole saltwater
fish such as bream or bass,
allow about 10 minutes
for every 2.5cm | 1 inch
in thickness, or about
20 minutes for every
500g | 1lb 2oz.

Whenever I make baked bream with potatoes, my husband says it reminds him of summer nights at my parent's home in Veneto, eating dinner under the pergola after a long day spent reading and snoozing at the beach.

Potatoes that have had time to cook under the saline juices of saltwater fish are in a league of their own. They gain flavour and tenderness and, at some point during the roasting process, they cease to be their own entity and become one with the fish. This is the sort of food I love to cook and eat: elemental and yet elegant, and as compelling as it is casual.

Preheat the oven to 200°C | 390°F | gas mark 6. Brush the bottom and sides of a large baking dish with olive oil. Slice the potatoes very thinly with a mandolin and arrange them in the dish, brushing each layer with oil and seasoning it with a pinch of salt and a turn of the pepper grinder. Cover with foil and bake for about 20 minutes.

Meanwhile, rinse the bream under cool running water and pat dry. Heat 1 tablespoon of olive oil in a large skillet and pan-fry the fish for 2 minutes per side. Remove from the heat and transfer into the baking dish, on top of the potatoes. Pour in the wine and cover with foil once again.

Bake the fish for 20 minutes, or until cooked all the way through (see Note left). Serve filleted, with the potatoes and a lemon wedge.

BRANZINO AL CARTOCCIO
Sea Bass Parcels

SERVES 4

60ml | ¼ cup extra virgin
olive oil

2 garlic cloves, whole but
lightly crushed

10–12 basil leaves,
roughly torn

2 large sea bass (about 500g
| 1lb 2oz each), cleaned
and filleted

Fine-grain sea salt and freshly
ground black pepper, to taste

1 unwaxed lemon

Note: I highly recommend the
tomato salad on page 95 as a
side to this lovely fish, as well
as a glass of crisp white wine.

I have a fondness for cooking fish al cartoccio *(enveloped in parcels of parchment paper). I like that all the juices remain nicely contained in a neat packet, and that the flavours multiply within it. I like that you can throw in just about anything — herbs, spices, chopped tomatoes, capers, olives, potatoes, julienned vegetables — and that they can play together, get acquainted, and hopefully work some wizardry.*

Bass is my fish of choice for cooking al cartoccio *because it has a sweet white flesh that remains moist and welcomes additional flavourings. Even in Venice and Chioggia, however, where the fish markets are big and the competition fierce, good bass is a treat, particularly wild-caught. Thankfully, there are some decent (extensively) farmed alternatives that are less impressive but cheaper and still good, and very much suited to this recipe.*

I make a few different versions of branzino al cartoccio *depending on the season. My favourite is perhaps the simplest, an all-season variant with just salt, pepper, garlic-and-basil-infused oil and a squeeze of lemon juice at the end.*

In a small bowl, whisk the oil with the garlic and basil. Cover tightly with cling film and leave to infuse for about 1 hour.

Preheat the oven to 180°C | 350°F | gas mark 4. Cut 4 squares of parchment (large enough to fit each fish fillet comfortably and make a parcel). On each place a bass fillet, skin-side down, drizzle with the flavoured oil and season with salt and pepper. Fold the paper, sealing the edges to make a parcel and tucking the ends underneath.

Bake until the fish is cooked through, 10–15 minutes, depending on the size of your fillet. Remove from the oven and serve the parcel, still closed, with lemon wedges on the side.

FOLPETTI E PATATE
Baby Octopus & Potato Salad

SERVES 3–4

1 teaspoon black peppercorns

2 bay leaves

750g | 1lb 10oz baby (musky) octopus, cleaned (see Note below) and tenderised

45ml | 3 tablespoons extra virgin olive oil

750g | 1lb 10oz (about 3 large) waxy potatoes, scrubbed

1 celery stick, trimmed and thinly sliced

Juice of 1 lemon

2 tablespoons very finely chopped flat-leaf parsley leaves

Fine-grain sea salt and freshly ground black pepper, to taste

Note: To clean the baby octopus yourself, remove the eyes, beak, internal cartilage and all the insides from the head. Wash them thoroughly under cold running water and pat dry before using. Or you can ask your fishmonger to do this for you.

In a not-so-hidden corner of Piazza della Frutta, in Padua, a small street stall selling seafood stretches out its red awning for l'ora dell'aperitivo, the happy hour. A hungry host of customers has already gathered. Some appear to be regulars, people who have made stopping at the stall part of their daily routine. They chat with the stall owners, Max and Barbara, while munching on their boiled seafood salad and sipping a glass of white. The owners seem to know exactly what they want and how much of it. They might give the regular a sneaky sconto (discount) — a courtesy reserved for few — but can't linger much in conversation. 'See you tomorrow,' they say, and move on to the next in the line. They'll only be there until the seafood lasts, and from the look of it, it won't last long.

Another look at the not-so-orderly queue reveals a few locals, not regulars but rather survivors from a strenuous session of sale shopping and in desperate need of a spur. They stop at the stall, starved, and reward themselves with a special something. 'What's good?' they ask. Everything. Everything is great. They order on a whim and then take their wobbly plate to the nearby bar to finally sit down, slip off their shoes, and summon a glass of prosecco.

By now, a curious couple — tourists, or perhaps day-trippers — have joined in, attracted by the crowds. They are new to the city, new to the rituals that envelope it and make it so enjoyable, so personable, despite the pretentious, provincial poise. They peek at what the locals are buying, make a mental note, and then, when their turn comes, they order timidly. 'We'll have two folpetti.' 'Bene,' says Max, scooping a bunch of boiled, curly baby octopus onto a paper plate. He cuts them into small chunks and then splashes them with some verdant parsley sauce. The newcomers look impressed. They pay and move to the side. I see them piercing a first piece of octopus with the toothpick, chew and utter a muffled moan. From the look of it, they'll be back.

CONTINUED OVERLEAF

I was a victim of the stall's temptations myself, first as a curious customer, then as a sporadic visitor, and finally as a completely addicted regular. Over the course of the three years I spent in Padua, I paid them an alarmingly high number of visits. I sampled pretty much the entire menu, but their folpi *(boiled musky octopus) remains what I go back for every time, whenever I'm in town.*

Octopus, big or small, can be a tough beast. It requires flash blanching or grilling, or else very long braises. A trick to make it more tender, aside from bashing it on the countertop or beating it up with a rock or a hammer, is to freeze it. The cold breaks down the tissues and helps make the meat less chewy. Some fishmongers might offer already-tenderised baby octopus, or — even better — cleaned and tenderised ones. Ask for advice and make sure they haven't been thawed already if you plan to make them sleep in the freezer. Size-wise, I always go for medium musky octopus (typical of the Adriatic), as tiny octopus isn't so tasty. If you struggle to find baby octopus, get a normal octopus, adjust the boiling time based on its size, then fry in chunks.

Bring a pan of water with the peppercorns and bay leaves to the boil. Stir in the octopus, cover and cook for 10-12 minutes, or until tender (the exact cooking time depends on the size of your octopus). Drain, discarding the aromatics, and set aside.

Heat 1 tablespoon of the olive oil in a large frying pan. When hot, add the octopus and sauté for 2-3 minutes, just enough for their skin to blister ever so slightly, and for the ends to curl up and become crispy. Season and set aside.

Meanwhile, boil the potatoes whole, skin on, until tender all the way through. Cool them under cold running water, then peel them and cut into smallish chunks. Arrange them on a serving platter together with the sliced celery. Make the dressing with the remaining olive oil, lemon juice and a generous pinch of salt and pour it over the potatoes; toss to coat. Place the baby octopus on top, sprinkle with the parsley and serve.

CALAMARI RIPIENI
Stuffed Squid

SERVES 4

12 small squid, cleaned,
  tentacles reserved

60ml | ¼ cup extra virgin olive
  oil, divided

2 garlic cloves, divided

60ml | ¼ cup dry white wine

100g | 3½oz crustless
  white bread

100g | 1 cup fine dry
  breadcrumbs

5 tablespoons very finely
  chopped flat-leaf
  parsley leaves

4 oil-packed anchovies,
  minced

Fine-grain sea salt and freshly
  ground black pepper, to taste

In a dark alley just past the Rialto Market is an osteria *that prepares the meanest calamari. They usually have them three ways: grilled, bearing delicious char marks on the pearly flesh; drenched in oregano-spiked red sauce; and stuffed. I usually have one of each, but as one always does with the best bite, I like leaving the stuffed squid for the very last.*

There are many schools of thoughts in relation to stuffed squid. Some grill it, basting it with oil and lemon; others bake it; and others again pan-fry it, either in tomato sauce or in bianco *(no sauce). I've used this last method here; by frying the stuffed squid over a vivacious flame you get flavour, tenderness and speed, all at the same time. The version I suggest has no sauce, though it includes a topping of crunchy, anchovy-flavoured breadcrumbs, creating a nice contrast of textures while also linking back to the flavours of the filling.*

Wash the squid thoroughly and pat dry; chop the tentacles very finely. Set aside.

In a small frying pan, heat half the olive oil and 1 garlic clove, whole but lightly crushed. Add the chopped tentacles and fry for 1 minute over a medium-high heat, until opaque. Pour in the wine and carry on cooking for 4–5 minutes, until the tentacles are tender and the liquid has evaporated completely. At this point, remove from the heat, discard the garlic and set aside to cool.

To make the stuffing, soak the white bread (lightly crumbed) in 2 tablespoons of water to soften, then squeeze out any excess liquid and place in a food processor together with the remaining grated garlic clove, three-quarters of the dry Italian breadcrumbs, 4 tablespoons of the parsley and 2 of the anchovies. Pulse until you have a coarse but even mixture. Combine it with the cooked tentacles and then refrigerate everything for 10 minutes.

CONTINUED OVERLEAF

Meanwhile, prepare the topping. Heat 1 tablespoon of olive oil in a small frying pan over a low heat and melt the remaining 2 anchovies in it, stirring until dissolved. Increase the heat, add the remaining of the fine breadcrumbs and fry, stirring often, until golden and fragrant, about 3 minutes.

Finally, take the squid bodies and fill them with the stuffing, then secure them with a couple of toothpicks. Heat the remaining 1 tablespoon of olive oil in a large frying pan over a medium-high heat. When hot, add the squid. Cook for 4–5 minutes each side, trying not to move them so that they can brown and char a little on the outside. Remove from the heat, top with the fried breadcrumbs and remaining 1 tablespoon of parsley and serve.

Slow-Cooked Beef Stew

SERVES 4

20g | 2¾ tablespoons plain
  flour, sifted

750g | 1lb 10oz beef chuck
  or rump roast, cut into 3cm
  | 1¼-inch chunks

30ml | 2 tablespoons extra
  virgin olive oil

1 golden onion, finely chopped

2 juniper berries

720ml | 3 cups beef stock,
  heated, plus more as needed

45ml | 3 tablespoons tomato
  sauce (passata)

Fine-grain sea salt and freshly
  ground black pepper, to taste

Note: To keep things regional,
I often serve *spezzatino* on
a bed of creamy polenta
(see pages 25–26), however,
consider mash (page 101) or
saucy peas (page 92), too.

* Horse meat and donkey
meat are part of Italy's
gastronomic heritage. They
are considered fine to eat in
most Italian regions, and
feature in many traditional
dishes.

I love everything about a good beef stew: the scent of browning meat wafting through the kitchen, the gentle bubbling, the comfort, and the many small sensations running down my spine as I see the meat melting at the touch of the fork. I love it because it's made with cheaper cuts, but by no means flavourless, only requiring more time and a bit of convincing to reveal their true, delightful self.

Venetians have never been huge consumers of beef, mostly because the raw material has for long been hard to obtain. Even when making a modest stew, we would choose other kinds of meats, such as veal, horse, or donkey.* This recipe, then, is a reinvented and yet rooted representation of the Venetian meat stew; a modern take on the classic as conceived in my Mum's heretical kitchen, and carried on in mine.

Flour the pieces of beef and transfer them to a sieve to shake off any excess flour. Set aside.

Heat the oil in a medium heavy-based pan. Add the onion and fry gently until soft and translucent, then remove. Increase the heat to medium-high and add the beef. Brown the meat on all sides (2–3 minutes per side), then put the onion back in, together with the juniper berries. Pour in the stock and the tomato sauce and scrape up the bits stuck to the bottom of the pan with a wooden spoon. Reduce the heat to low and cover with a lid.

Cook for 2½–3 hours, or until the liquid has boiled down to a thick sauce and the meat is extremely tender. Check and adjust the seasoning and add a little more stock or water during the cooking time if you see that the sauce is reducing too quickly.

Once ready, remove the stew from the heat and leave it to rest for 10 minutes before serving.

Beef Pot Roast with Parsley Sauce

SERVES 4

For the bollito:

1kg | 2lb 3oz braising beef
  (brisket or blade)
2 carrots, peeled
1 celery stick, trimmed
Small bunch of flat-leaf parsley
1 golden onion, quartered
3 bay leaves
1 teaspoon black peppercorns
Fine-grain sea salt, to taste

For the salsa verde:

50g | 1¾oz crustless
  white bread
100ml | ⅓ cup + 1 tablespoon
  white wine vinegar
100g | 3½oz flat-leaf
  parsley leaves
20g | ¾oz capers, rinsed
3 small cornichons, sliced
2 hard-boiled egg yolks
6 oil-packed anchovy fillets,
  drained and chopped
1 garlic clove, sliced
120ml | ½ cup extra virgin
  olive oil, plus more as needed

Note: Leftovers can be used to
forge a batch of rissoles (see
page 144). A few serving ideas:
hot, with *salsa verde*, alongside
a bowl of buttery potato mash
or potato salad; in a sandwich,
cold, with more *salsa verde*.

Bollito misto *is a wintry feast of boiled meats in which beef (in the form of lesser cuts) makes an appearance alongside veal,* cotechino *(a fresh sausage of pork scraps, pork rind and spices), and chicken. This is conventionally served with the holy trinity of traditional sauces: salsa verde (parsley sauce), cren (horseradish sauce) and mostarda veneta (a concoction of candied fruits preserved in a mustardy syrup).*

Of the bollito misto *banquet, I'm sharing my preferred part: the boiled beef with the* salsa verde. *It's a dish that suits each and every season, for it's as delicious hot as it is cold.*

Place all the ingredients for the *bollito* in a large pan. Cover with water so that the meat is completely submerged and set the pan over a medium heat. Once the liquid has reached the boil, reduce the heat to a simmer and cook for about 3 hours. Check it every 30 minutes, skimming off the scum that rises to the surface and topping up with water so that the meat is always covered in liquid. Halfway through, taste the liquid and adjust the seasoning.

When time is up, poke the meat with a fork: if it feels giving and tender all the way through, it's done. Remove from the heat and allow the meat to rest in its cooking liquid while you make the sauce.

For the *salsa verde*, soak the white bread in vinegar for 5 minutes. Squeeze out the liquid and then place the bread in a food processor or the container of a hand-held stick blender together with the rest of the ingredients. Blitz and blend until smooth and creamy, adding a little more oil if needed, until you reach a silky texture.

When ready to serve, gently remove the meat from the liquid and cut it into slices — they won't be neat but that's okay. Serve warm or at room temperature, alongside a spoonful or two of *salsa verde*.

GALLINA UBRIACA
Hen in Red Wine

SERVES 6

1 medium free-range chicken
(about 1.5kg | 3lb 5oz),
cleaned and cut into 8 pieces

40g | ⅓ cup plain flour

30ml | 2 tablespoons extra
virgin olive oil

2 garlic cloves, whole but
lightly crushed

60ml | ¼ cup brandy

1 bottle (750ml) full-bodied
Merlot or Cabernet, plus
more as needed

200g | 7oz white or brown
button mushrooms

30g | 2 tablespoons
unsalted butter

100g | 3½oz piece of flat
pancetta, minced

2 golden onions, finely
chopped

Fine-grain sea salt and freshly
ground black pepper, to taste

If you've never come across a gallina padovana, *I encourage you to do a web search: it's one of the poshest, funniest-looking feathery animals I've ever seen. And, as it turns out, one of the tastiest, too.*

I discovered the existence of this rare breed when I first moved to Padua. The poultry shops of the food hall under the arches of the Palazzo della Ragione would sometimes carry them, often advertising their presence in big letters, as if they were guest stars. The fact that gallina padovana *is a protected breed, honoured by the Slow Food Presidium, explains their celebrity status. These hens are indeed reared in the best possible conditions. They roam freely in the verdant gardens of the hills surrounding the city. They are happy, beautiful birds — veracious, muscly, and (as I would soon realise) full of flavour.*

With such a reputation for — and wealth of — quality poultry, the culinary repertoire of Padua is not short on chicken recipes. Among them, the recipe for gallina ubriaca *(drunk hen) is perhaps the most representative. The* gallina *— a nicely sized* ruspante *(farmyard) specimen — is cooked slowly and purposefully in red wine (often originating from the same hills) until the meat is about to fall off the bone. The wine bubbles down to a delightful gravy — dark and juicy, dotted with fat. The accompaniment of pancetta, onions and mushrooms, cooked separately and added at the very last moment, delivers yet more flavour — as if it was needed — and a scrumptious umami blast.*

Note: In order to make the dish a tad lighter, I sometimes remove the skin from the chicken's breast and thighs, but leave it on the drumsticks and wings. This is especially valid when the skin is particularly thick (a common feature in farmyard chickens). Ultimately, it's up to you — it all depends on the type of bird you're dealing with. Once again, this dish is great served with polenta; but if you're tired of it, mashed potatoes (see page 101) and stir-fried greens (see pages 90 and 209) are both excellent alternatives.

Roll the chicken pieces in flour and shake off any excess. Heat the oil in a large, heavy-based pan, add the garlic and leave it to infuse the oil for a couple of minutes, until fragrant, then discard it. Add the chicken pieces and brown them on all sides, trying not to move them too much so that they can form a crisp crust. Now, pour in the brandy and allow it to evaporate, scraping at the tasty bits that are stuck on the bottom of the pan. Season with salt and pepper, pour in the wine, then reduce the heat and place a lid on top.

Cook the chicken for about 1½ hours. By then, the meat should feel extremely tender and be almost falling off the bone. Check that the sauce doesn't reduce too quickly; top it up with a little more wine if that's the case.

Meanwhile, brush off any dirt from the mushrooms using a damp towel. Trim the stalks and slice them thinly; set aside.

In a large frying pan, melt the butter and fry the pancetta over a medium heat. Add the onions and cook until very soft, stirring often. Now, add the mushrooms and increase the heat. Sauté for 3–4 minutes over a vivacious heat; season and then reduce the heat to medium and cook until their liquid has reduced.

When there are 10 minutes left before removing the chicken from the heat, stir in the mushroom mixture and finish cooking it all together over a low heat. Taste the sauce and adjust the seasoning if needed, then turn off the heat and leave to rest for 30 minutes, or, ideally, for a couple of hours. Warm it up again, taste and adjust the seasoning before serving.

Meatballs in Tomato Sauce

SERVES 4–6 / MAKES 25
MEDIUM OR 30 SMALL
MEATBALLS

60g | 2oz crustless white
  bread
60ml | ¼ cup whole milk
450g | 1lb minced beef
150g | 5¼oz minced pork
1 egg, lightly beaten
25g | ¼ cup fine dry
  breadcrumbs
1 garlic clove, grated
3 tablespoons very finely
  chopped flat-leaf
  parsley leaves
Fine-grain sea salt and freshly
  ground black pepper, to taste

For the sauce:
2 × 400g | 2 × 14oz tins
  peeled plum tomatoes
  (San Marzano or Roma)
30ml | 2 tablespoons extra
  virgin olive oil
½ golden onion, very finely
  chopped
1 teaspoon granulated sugar
  (optional)
¼ teaspoon bicarbonate
  of soda (optional)
Fine-grain sea salt, to taste
A little vegetable stock,
  as needed

Aunt Maria Teresa is the kind of cook everyone in the family looks up to. Born in the early 1950s, her cooking is vintage, inspired by the well-seasoned array of dishes passed down through her family; her repertoire is small but consistent, her food always unfailingly good.

Of Aunt's many specialities, her meatballs have always had my vote. Different from the shallow-fried meatballs of Venetian tradition, hers are braised in a velvety, sweet, zingy tomato sauce, which in turn imparts juiciness and flavour to the meat. On the side, a generous scoop of mashed potatoes would often make an appearance. For my young self, it just didn't get any better than that; it still doesn't.

———————

In a small bowl, soak the white bread (loosely crumbed) in the milk until softened, about 2 minutes. Squeeze out any excess liquid and transfer the crumbs to a separate, larger bowl. Add both meats and the egg and mix until evenly combined. Stir in the breadcrumbs, garlic, parsley, a dash of salt and a generous dose of pepper and mix again. Cover the bowl with cling film and allow to rest in the fridge for 1 hour.

To make the sauce, pass the contents of the tomato tins through a food mill placed over a bowl. Alternatively, press the tomatoes through a metal sieve. In a large frying pan, heat the olive oil over a medium heat. Add the onion and fry gently until soft and translucent. Pour in the tomatoes, reduce the heat and allow it to simmer for about 15 minutes, until dense and silky. Taste and season; add a little sugar, if the sauce is too bland, or the tip of a teaspoon of bicarbonate of soda if too acidic — it all depends on the type of tomatoes.

Take the meat mix out of the fridge and start shaping it into meatballs as big as a large walnut. Add to the frying pan with the sauce and cook them for 5 minutes each side, or until cooked through. If the sauce reduces excessively, add a splash of hot vegetable stock. Serve right away.

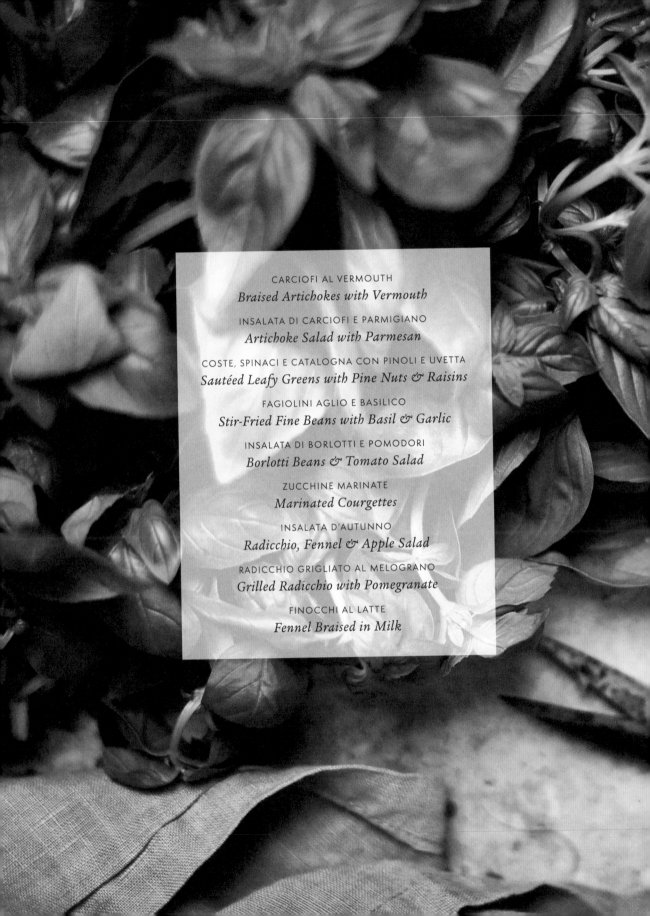

CARCIOFI AL VERMOUTH
Braised Artichokes with Vermouth

INSALATA DI CARCIOFI E PARMIGIANO
Artichoke Salad with Parmesan

COSTE, SPINACI E CATALOGNA CON PINOLI E UVETTA
Sautéed Leafy Greens with Pine Nuts & Raisins

FAGIOLINI AGLIO E BASILICO
Stir-Fried Fine Beans with Basil & Garlic

INSALATA DI BORLOTTI E POMODORI
Borlotti Beans & Tomato Salad

ZUCCHINE MARINATE
Marinated Courgettes

INSALATA D'AUTUNNO
Radicchio, Fennel & Apple Salad

RADICCHIO GRIGLIATO AL MELOGRANO
Grilled Radicchio with Pomegranate

FINOCCHI AL LATTE
Fennel Braised in Milk

CONTORNI

Braised Artichokes with Vermouth

SERVES 4

12 medium violet artichokes
(see Notes below and
overleaf)
2 lemons
45ml | 3 tablespoons extra
virgin olive oil
60ml | ¼ cup white vermouth
(or white wine, or a mix)
Fine-grain sea salt and freshly
ground black pepper, to taste
8–10 mint or calamint leaves,
to serve (optional)

If there's one recipe that caught my eye as soon as I began cooking from Elizabeth David's brilliant book, Italian Food, *it has to be that for carciofi alla veneziana. I made that recipe an uncountable number of times, and tweaked it just as many. The most successful of these tweaks happened one night when, already halfway through the artichoke cleaning process, I realised all I had to cook with was a half-drunk bottle of white vermouth. I used that instead of wine, and have never looked back.*

The vermouth does an excellent job in subduing the mild astringency of the artichokes. It enhances their natural sweetness while also imparting a vague herbal note that is extremely pleasant. As the cooking liquids reduce, the sugars in the vermouth caramelise to form a sticky sauce that coats the artichokes and makes them shine beautifully.

Note: When buying artichokes, look for very tight leaves, and for firmness from the base all the way to the top. It's always a good thing when they come with a longer stem and the leaves still attached — often a sign of greater freshness. These artichokes make a fantastic side to fresh cheeses such as ricotta, casatella and even burrata.

Soak the artichokes in water for 30 minutes. Rinse, drain and pat dry.

Using a serrated knife, halve the lemons and squeeze some juice on the blade. Remove the outer leaves of the artichokes until you reach the pale, tender, inner ones. Trim the stalk 3cm | 1¼ inches from the base and peel it to reveal the white core. Cut off any hard bit at the base and then trim the ends of the remaining leaves. Cut the artichokes in quarters and scoop out and discard the hairy choke. At every stage, rub the cut parts with a slice of lemon to avoid discoloration.

Heat the oil in a large frying pan. Add the artichokes and sauté for a couple of minutes over a medium heat. Pour in the vermouth and allow it to evaporate. Next, pour in 120ml | ½ cup water, reduce the heat and cover. Braise the artichokes for about 20 minutes, or until they feel tender when pierced with a fork.

Uncover, season with salt and pepper, then increase the heat again and let the cooking juices reduce to a light brown, sticky sauce, stirring often. Remove from the heat and sprinkle with calamint or some roughly torn mint leaves if you like.

Artichoke Salad with Parmesan

SERVES 4

8 violet artichokes (see Notes
   below and on page 206)
2 lemons
30ml | 2 tablespoons extra
   virgin olive oil
50g | 1¾oz Parmesan, shaved
Flaky sea salt and freshly
   ground black pepper, to taste

Note: Aside from this
particular variety of artichoke,
others that are good raw are
the spiky variety from Liguria
or from Sardinia, and the
very young *Petit Violet.* Opt
for artichokes that are young,
fresh and extremely tender,
with tight leaves, a firm base
and very little hairy 'choke' at
the centre.

At the far end of the Venetian lagoon is the remote island of Sant'Erasmo. Locals call it the garden of Venice; it has long functioned as a vegetable garden supplying fresh produce to the city. To this day, Sant'Erasmo remains peaceful and bucolic. Its landscape is still dotted by vegetable patches, big and small, messy and tidy.

Of the many delights that ripen on the island, the artichoke carciofo violetto di Sant'Erasmo *is perhaps the most remarkable. Not only does it look like a purple rose blossom, but it also has a flavour and tenderness equal to none. Inside its pretty berry-tinted leaves are a delicate heart and a sweet spirit, balanced by a hint of bitterness that is anything but blatant. It's impossible not to fall in love.*

Carciofo violetto *works in just about everything artichokes can work in — braises, stews, stir-fries, omelettes, risottos, soups and so on. And yet I think the best way to enjoy it is raw, thinly sliced and tossed with a generous splash of green, peppery olive oil and a squeeze of lemon juice, and finished with a few shavings of Parmesan. Serve it with grilled fish or steak and you're in for a real treat.*

Soak the artichokes in water for 30 minutes. Rinse, drain and pat dry.

Using a serrated knife, halve the lemons and squeeze some juice on the blade. Remove the outer leaves, of the artichokes until you reach the pale, tender, inner ones. Trim the stalk 3cm | 1¼ inches from the base and peel it to reveal the white core. Cut off any hard bit at the base and then trim the ends of the remaining leaves. Cut the artichokes in half and scoop out and discard the hairy choke; slice very thinly. At every stage, rub the cut parts with lemon to avoid discoloration and then squeeze some lemon juice over the artichoke slices.

Place the artichokes in a bowl and drizzle with the oil. Season with a generous pinch of crushed flaky sea salt and a good dose of black pepper and toss. Arrange on a plate and top with the shaved Parmesan. Serve.

Sautéed Leafy Greens with Pine Nuts & Raisins

SERVES 4–6

750g | 1lb 10oz (about 1 large head) Swiss chard

750g | 1lb 10oz (about 1 large head) chicory

300g | 10½oz (about 1 large bunch) spinach

60ml | ¼ cup extra virgin olive oil

3 garlic cloves, whole but lightly crushed

40g | ¼ cup raisins

40g | ¼ cup pine nuts, toasted

Fine-grain sea salt, to taste

In winter, every stall in the bustling market of Padua's Piazza delle Erbe carries piles of bunched leaves: hearty spinach with large crumpled leaves and pale pink roots; sturdy, shiny Swiss chard heads, pearl-white at the core but otherwise forest-green; and pointy chicory, always too big to fit in my bicycle basket and too bitter to eat on its own.

When these are in season, I often find myself dining on little else. Stir fried, studded with pine nuts and raisins, they make for a fulfilling yet stupidly simple meal, especially when served alongside some good aged cheese (Piave Vecchio or Asiago Mezzano come to mind), a hunk of crusty bread and a glass of red wine.

Wash the greens in plenty of cold water until you see no signs of dirt and grit. Trim the roots and chop the leaves and stalks into 2.5cm | 1-inch pieces.

Bring a large pan of salted water to the boil. Add the chopped greens and boil for 7–8 minutes, or until the stems have just lost their crudeness. Drain in a colander to release excess liquid, squeezing them down to help with the process — placing a weight on top helps.

Place a large frying pan with the oil over a medium heat. Add the garlic and fry gently until fragrant but not browned. (You can remove it after it has infused the oil. I leave it in.) Add the greens and increase the heat to medium-high. Season, toss, taste and adjust to your liking.

Stir-fry for 8–10 minutes, until the greens appear shiny and soft but the stems are still crunchy. At this point, add the raisins and pine nuts, toss once more and then remove from the heat. Serve warm.

Stir-Fried Fine Beans with Basil & Garlic

SERVES 4

400g | 14oz fine beans, ends
    trimmed
30ml | 2 tablespoons extra
    virgin olive oil
5 garlic cloves, whole but
    lightly crushed
8–10 basil leaves
Flaky sea salt and freshly
    ground black pepper, to taste

For as long as summer lasts, there never seems to be a shortage of green beans in my family kitchen: the garden keeps giving and giving. Mum prepares them two ways: blanched and tossed with lemon and oil, or else stir-fried with basil and garlic. We all seem to have a soft spot for this last option, a preference that has remained strong throughout the years.

Conscious of the reputation Italians have for cooking green beans to death, I am keen to say that this isn't the case in this recipe. In fact, though they go through two stages of cooking (boiled and stir-fried), their time in the frying pan actually improves their texture, and adds flavour while at it. Garlic and basil make the beans more succulent, though much of their goodness resides in their lightly charred skins — achieved by means of a very hot pan and some well-timed tossing — and in the thin film of aromatic oil coating them as they glide from pan to plate.

It is fairly important that the beans are small and snappy, though if they just look a bit sad they can be revived in an icy bath for an hour prior to cooking. Don't be intimidated by the large amount of garlic in this dish: by leaving the cloves crushed but whole you'll have all the delicious pungency without the harshness. I like serving these next to a wide array of summery foods such as prosciutto, bresaola, carpaccio, mozzarella — plus plenty of good bread, of course.

Bring a large pan of water to the boil. Add the beans and cook, uncovered, for 4–5 minutes, or until just tender and bright green in colour. Drain and plunge into really cold water to halt the cooking.

Meanwhile, heat the oil and garlic in a large frying pan. Allow the garlic to gain a golden complexion, then add the well-drained beans. Stir-fry over a high heat, moving them every couple of minutes and allowing their skin to char and blister on all sides.

At the very end, stir in the basil leaves and season with salt and pepper. Sauté the beans for another minute and then serve.

Borlotti Beans & Tomato Salad

SERVES 4–6

1kg | 2lb 3oz borlotti beans
in the pods (see Note
below), shelled

45ml | 3 tablespoons extra
virgin olive oil

1 red onion, thinly sliced

3 medium bull's heart
tomatoes, at room
temperature

1 teaspoon white wine vinegar

3 tablespoons roughly
chopped flat-leaf
parsley leaves

Fine-grain sea salt, to taste

Note: Veneto grows some
magnificent (PDO) beans
in the area of Lamon, near
Belluno. Fresh, they reveal
a unique nutty, creamy soul
that lends itself to all sorts
of preparations, particularly
salads. Having said that, you
can use any fresh borlotti
variety as long as they are
good. If it comes to the worst,
you can also substitute dried
borlotti (prepared as described
on pages 47 and 48) though
the result will be slightly less
sprightly.

When summer's sweltering heat hits the flatlands of Veneto, I shut off the stove and live off salads, fresh cheeses, bread and watermelon. My summer salads vary in substance and colour, but usually start with a few ripe bull's heart tomatoes. Adding beans and aromatics turns them into quick, light, fresh one-bowl meals.

Thinly sliced red onion makes for a good sidekick to beans and tomatoes; so does parsley, whose agreement with beans is indisputable. Flavours and textures, so important in a good salad, are in balance: you have zingy, umami, fresh, nutty, creamy, piquant and crisp, all in one bowl. In this sense, this salad would be perfectly at ease served alone, perhaps with bread and a piece of cheese on the side; though it will also make a nice complement to other summery salads, or a fine picnic idea.

Put the shelled beans in a large pan with cold water to cover. Set the pan over a medium heat and bring to the boil. Reduce the heat to a simmer and cook, partially covered, for about 40 minutes, or until the beans are tender but still holding their shape. Every now and then, check the water level and add more if needed; skim off any foam that comes to the surface. Drain, season with 15ml | 1 tablespoon of oil and a generous pinch of salt. Leave to cool.

Soak the onion in cold water for 10 minutes, then drain and set aside. Cut the tomatoes into segments and scatter them on a large salad plate. Whisk the remaining 30ml | 2 tablespoons of oil with the vinegar and a dash of salt until well combined. Pour the dressing over the tomatoes and toss to coat. Top with the cooled beans, onion slices and chopped parsley. Toss again, taste, and adjust the seasoning to your liking. Serve at room temperature.

Marinated Courgettes

SERVES 3–4

800g | 1lb 12oz small
  courgettes
60ml | ¼ cup white wine
  vinegar
60ml | ¼ cup water
3 garlic cloves, thinly sliced
Sunflower oil, for frying
10–12 mint leaves
Fine-grain sea salt and freshly
  ground black pepper, to taste

Note: For this dish, use small
courgettes with a tight flesh
and few seeds; they'll dry
faster and will absorb less oil
when frying.

*Fried, marinated courgettes became a favourite from the very first time
I tasted them in a restaurant in the Colli Euganei. I remember being
struck by their complexity, swinging from sour to sweet, garlicky and yet
fresh, tender and chewy. I have been making them regularly ever since
— every year, from late spring to the end of summer — using the tiniest
fresh courgettes I can find.*

*At home, I like serving these courgettes as a side to poached mackerel (see
page 184), a glass of white wine, and bread to mop up the marinade.*

Slice the courgettes into discs of 2–3mm | 0.1 inch. Arrange the slices
on a tea towel and cover with another towel. Let them rest for at least
1 hour to drain. Meanwhile, place the vinegar and water in a small pan
and bring to the boil. Add the garlic and allow the liquid to reduce to
about half its volume. Remove from the heat and cover to keep warm.

Fill two-thirds of a medium, high-sided frying pan with sunflower oil.
Place it over a medium-high heat, and wait until it reaches a temperature
of 180°C | 350°F, which you can test with a thermometer or by inserting
the handle of a wooden spoon in the oil; when small but fierce bubbles
form around it, it's ready. Fry the courgettes in batches until golden and
a bit wrinkly. Drain with a slotted spoon and transfer to a plate covered
with kitchen paper. Season every batch with a pinch of salt and plenty
of freshly ground black pepper.

Transfer the courgettes to a jar or a glass bowl. Alternate each layer of
courgettes with a few roughly torn mint leaves. Pour over the warm
marinade and then leave to cool to room temperature. Once cold, close
the jar (or cover the bowl with cling film) and place it in the fridge. Allow
the courgettes to rest overnight before eating them.

Radicchio, Fennel & Apple Salad

SERVES 4

1 small head of Rosa di
Castelfranco, or use
round radicchio

3 small bunches of red or
green baby wild radicchio
(grumolo), or use red endive
and green endive

80g | 3½oz rocket

150g | 5¼oz (about 1 small)
fennel

1 small snappy apple, thinly
sliced

Juice of ½ lemon

30ml | 2 tablespoons extra
virgin olive oil

15ml | 1 tablespoon white
wine vinegar

Fine-grain sea salt, to taste

Note: I like to serve this salad
either at the start of the meal,
followed by risotto or another
creamy main; or as a side to
roasted chicken or guinea
fowl (see page 72). In terms
of radicchio varieties, the
common, round chioggiotto
can replace one or both
kinds (Castelfranco and
grumolo), though these are
worth seeking out for their
unique flavour profile and
appearance.

*In winter, not a day went by without a bowl of shivering-bitter radicchio
salad making an appearance on our family table. The salad often consisted
of radicchio alone, or perhaps a medley of varieties. On occasion, a few
other cold-season leaves and vegetables would creep in, too — peppery
rocket, paper-thin fennel shavings, perhaps some finely shredded cabbage
or a couple of grated carrots. In recent times sliced apple, pear and
pomegranate seeds have also begun to make sporadic appearances.*

*Of all the variations on this theme, the combination of rocket, fennel and
apple has always been my favourite. Radicchio remains the backbone
of the bowl. It features in two forms: the speckled Rosa di Castelfranco,
with its ample, buttery leaves, and the small but mighty wild radicchio
— multi-coloured, poignant and piercingly astringent. On the flavour
front, rocket adds heat, while the apple adds sugar. Finally, fennel gives
snap, structure and crunch, and a vague spiced sweetness that is at ease
with the bitter base of the leaves.*

Cut off the roots of the radicchio, wash the leaves thoroughly and spin
dry in a salad spinner. Break the leaves roughly and place them into a
large bowl. Do the same with the rocket, but keep the leaves whole.

Wash the fennel; discard the outer layer if it's tough or blemished.
Trim the tops, reserving the green fronds for later. Slice it very thinly,
either with a mandolin or using a very sharp knife. Place in a small bowl
together with the apple slices, squeeze some lemon juice on them and
toss to coat (this will make sure they stay white). Scatter over the salad
leaves and set aside.

Whisk the oil with vinegar and a couple of pinches of salt. Pour it over
the salad and toss until evenly seasoned. Top with a few fennel fronds
and serve.

RADICCHIO GRIGLIATO AL MELOGRANO
Grilled Radicchio with Pomegranate

SERVES 4

60ml | ¼ cup pomegranate
  juice*
30ml | 2 tablespoons extra
  virgin olive oil
15ml | 1 tablespoon good-
  quality balsamic vinegar
1 teaspoon dark brown sugar
600g | 1lb 5oz (about 2 heads)
  radicchio trevisano or
  tardivo (see Note below)
Fine-grain sea salt, to taste

Note: Choose the elongated
trevisano or the mild tardivo
over salad varieties for this
dish, as they stand up better
to grilling.

* Made by juicing the seeds of
1 small pomegranate. I peel
and seed a pomegranate, then
press the seeds through a very
fine sieve set over a bowl to
collect their juice.

*I won't bore you with the trite and over-quoted Proust madeleine story
here, however, I can't help but be constantly amazed at how powerful
the senses (and food) can be in relation to our memory. It happens to
me every time I spend a good 15 minutes hunched over a bowl of water,
seeding pomegranates. It's a relaxing process, therapeutic really; there's
no room for impatience and the slowness of it must be embraced. In it
I find the ideal situation for daydreaming and recollection and I often
find myself thinking back to the time I drove across northern Italy with a
car full of pomegranates — fruits rolling all over the back seat and seeds
sneaking out of the many cracks, bursting in bright pink Pollock-style
spatters all over the upholstery.*

*It was October a few years ago. I was on my way back to Piedmont after
a weekend spent visiting my family. Before hitting the road, I went to say
goodbye to Grandma and found her busy packing enough provisions to
survive a Siberian winter: bag after bag of garden vegetables, two dozen
eggs (neatly wrapped in newspaper and placed inside a shoebox), a bag
of walnuts from a nearby farm, jarred tomatoes, and a box filled with
pomegranates from her tree. I asked her whether she wanted to keep any
of these; she said she didn't have much patience for cracking and seeding
them. And so, greedy as I was, I took them all.*

*Later that day, driving across the foggy flatlands of Veneto, I caught sight
of a few fields where seasonal pickers were digging radicchio, easily the
main autumnal crop in the area. Awfully bitter while also invigorating,
it is one of the flavours I love the most about my homeland. Suddenly
eager to buy some to take with me, I turned my car around — that's
when the first spillage of pomegranate happened — and liberated the
local greengrocer of much of his daily stock of radicchio. I then spent
the following four-hour drive worrying about the pomegranate situation,
and pondering about dinner.*

*The fruit of this pondering is, among other things, this simple radicchio
recipe. I like to think of it as a celebration of autumn and its fruits as
they grow in my homeland, but also as a symphony of flavours that
happen to go really well together. Radicchio and pomegranate are bound
by contrast and balance. The sweet and sour notes of the fruit soften*

the bitterness of the vegetable and create a delicious sticky glaze when heated. Balsamic vinegar only plays a supporting role here, yet is crucial to mellow things further and paint a deep burgundy, autumnal tint to the ensemble.

First, prepare your glaze by whisking together the pomegranate juice with oil, balsamic vinegar, sugar and a pinch of salt.

Next, wash the radicchio and pat it dry with a clean towel. Quarter the heads, then remove the hard part of the root while still keeping enough for the leaves to hold together. Place the radicchio wedges on a plate. Brush their whole surface with the glaze, then let them sit for 15 minutes to absorb part of the marinade.

Place a non-stick griddle pan over a medium-high heat. When hot, add the radicchio quarters and a bit of their marinade. Griddle the radicchio for 3–4 minutes on each side, until tender and cooked through. Remove from the heat and arrange on a serving platter, including any leftover cooking juices. Serve warm.

FINOCCHI AL LATTE
Fennel Braised in Milk

SERVES 4

750g | 1lb 10oz (about
   3 medium bulbs) fennel,
   trimmed (see Note right)
30g | 2 tablespoons unsalted
   butter, plus more for the
   baking tray
1 litre | 4¼ cups whole milk
Freshly grated nutmeg
   (optional)
50g | 1¾oz Grana Padano,
   grated
Fine-grain sea salt, to taste

Fennel cooked in milk is a delight I came to discover later in life — while in Padua and well on the path to becoming the sort of food fanatic who then moves to a tiny village to study gastronomy.

My then-boyfriend and I had been invited for dinner with another student couple. As soon as we arrived, the guy — a goofy but smart kid from the nearby mountains — stuck a glass of prosecco in our hands with perfect Venetian hospitality. His girlfriend, a petite girl from Sicily, greeted us from the other room. She was pottering around the stove, haloed by a haze of cooking vapours. I headed towards the kitchen to say hello, but mainly to peek at the pots and pans bubbling away. A pan with fennel simmering in a pale liquid immediately caught my attention. 'Finocchi al latte,' she announced, a recipe she had brought with her from her hometown of Trapani. It sounded and smelled divine.

The idea of fennel cooked in milk fogged my thoughts for the rest of the evening. I was so eager to taste it, so fixated on it, that I hardly remember the rest of the meal — what we ate, what we said. All I recall is its arrival at the table and the certainty, after a first bite, that it was the best fennel I'd ever had. Its structure had relaxed in the braising process, giving way to a delightful melt-in-the mouth feel, while the milk had muted the anise note, turning it into a more gentle, clean sweetness. It was pure delight.

Although I was too stupidly shy to ask for the recipe, in time I managed to master the method, twisting it and tuning it to my own taste. This is how the recipe stands to date, the most remarkable difference to the original being that my braised fennel is then covered in grated cheese and broiled until crisp, golden and — as I see it — plain irresistible.

Note: Choosing good fennel can be a tricky matter. Season-wise, fennel tends to be at its best during the cooler months. Shape can provide guidance, too: opt for the squat, rounder bulbs (males) rather than the long, thin ones (females); the former are often more tender, sweeter, with fewer strings and a more intense anise scent.

Preheat the oven to 180°C | 350°F | gas mark 4.

Cut the trimmed fennel bulbs into 8 segments each. Melt the butter in a large pan and, when hot and bubbly, add the fennel. Move the pieces around so that they are coated in fat. Allow them to cook gently for 5 minutes over a medium heat, stirring often, and then pour in the milk, season with nutmeg, if using, and salt, reduce the heat to low and cover with a lid.

Cook the fennel for about 20 minutes, or until tender and cooked through but still holding its shape. Drain with a slotted spoon and transfer to a buttered baking tray big enough to host the fennel in a single layer. Pour in a bit of the cooking liquid — about 120ml | ½ cup — and sprinkle the top with the Parmesan.

Bake in the oven until the liquid has reduced, about 10 minutes. Towards the end, turn the oven to the grill function and grill for 2–3 minutes, enough for the top to brown and turn crisp. Serve.

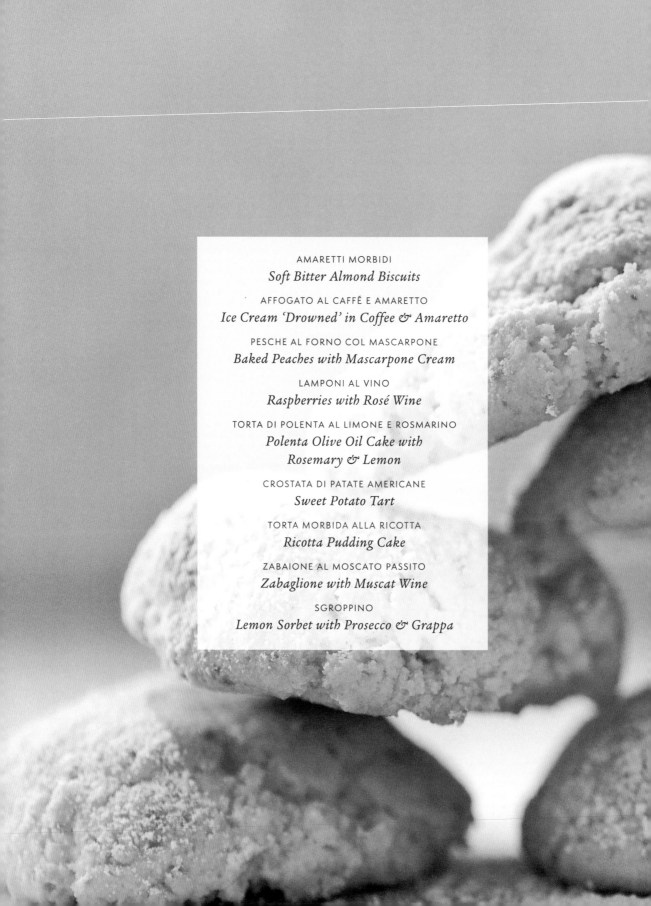

AMARETTI MORBIDI
Soft Bitter Almond Biscuits

AFFOGATO AL CAFFÉ E AMARETTO
Ice Cream 'Drowned' in Coffee & Amaretto

PESCHE AL FORNO COL MASCARPONE
Baked Peaches with Mascarpone Cream

LAMPONI AL VINO
Raspberries with Rosé Wine

TORTA DI POLENTA AL LIMONE E ROSMARINO
*Polenta Olive Oil Cake with
Rosemary & Lemon*

CROSTATA DI PATATE AMERICANE
Sweet Potato Tart

TORTA MORBIDA ALLA RICOTTA
Ricotta Pudding Cake

ZABAIONE AL MOSCATO PASSITO
Zabaglione with Muscat Wine

SGROPPINO
Lemon Sorbet with Prosecco & Grappa

DOLCI

AMARETTI MORBIDI
Soft Bitter Almond Biscuits

MAKES ABOUT 20

20g | ¾oz dry apricot kernels
(or use 20g | ¾oz ground
almonds plus 1½ teaspoons
almond extract)

200g | 1¾ cups icing sugar,
sifted, plus more for rolling
and dusting

180g | 1¾ cups + 1 tablespoon
ground almonds

70g | 2½oz (about 2)
egg whites

Note: Apricot kernels, or else
bitter almonds (*armelline*),
are definitely worth seeking
out for this recipe. They are
known for being poisonous
when ingested in large
amounts, but the dose listed
here is far from lethal. If you
can't find them, a few drops
of almond extract make a fine
substitution; just use more
ground almonds to make up
for the weight difference.

Sometimes wrapped in colourful tissue paper, sometimes in vintage-looking metal tins, these tender-crumbed almond biscuits appear in the baking tradition of many Italian regions, especially Liguria and Lombardy. In Venice, the tradition is likely acquired, though it found a perfect fit in the city's time-honoured passion for crafting almond-based sweets.

Akin to Sicilian pasta di mandorle, *the greatness of soft amaretti rests on the fragile equilibrium between the tender heart and the crumbly crystallised shell; the intense, marzipan-like sugariness and the contrasting notes of bitter almonds. Whether served alongside a bowl of zabaglione, crumbled over ice cream or crushed on baked peaches (see pages 244–246, 228 and 231), these will be in their element.*

In a food processor or spice grinder, grind the apricot kernels together with 1 tablespoon of the icing sugar until you have a fine meal. (Or mix the 20g | ¾oz ground almonds and the almond extract.) Transfer to a large bowl and add the 180g | 1¾ cups + 1 tablespoon of ground almonds and the rest of the sugar. Stir to combine.

In a smaller glass or metal bowl, beat the egg whites to stiff peaks. Fold them into the dry ingredients until it all comes together into a sticky but even ball of dough. Cover the bowl with cling film and refrigerate for 1 hour.

Next, preheat the oven to 180°C | 350°F | gas mark 4 and line a baking tray with parchment. Scoop a scant tablespoon of dough (about 20g | ¾oz) and work it between your palms to form a ball. Roll it in icing sugar, shake off any excess, flatten it slightly and ease it on to the lined baking tray. Repeat with the rest. Ensure a couple of centimetres between each biscuit — if 1 tray is not enough, bake in 2 batches, keeping the remaining dough in the fridge while the first batch bakes.

Place the tray in the upper middle part of the oven. Bake for 18 minutes, or until golden and wrinkly. Transfer to a rack to cool completely. Store in an airtight container or metal tin for up to 2 weeks.

Ice Cream 'Drowned' in Coffee & Amaretto

SERVES 4

60ml | ¼ cup amaretto
liqueur
500g | 18oz almond ice cream
(see Note below)
8 amaretti biscuits (see page
227 or use shop-bought)
4 shots of strong espresso
(or use 180ml | ¾ cup
hot Moka-pot coffee)

Note: If you're not keen
on my 'everything almond'
take, most creamy/nutty
flavours (such as vanilla,
hazelnut, pistachio etc.) will
naturally work here. The only
aspect to pay attention to is
the coffee, which should be
piping hot when poured into
the glasses in order to melt
the ice cream and create the
desired puddle effect.

Affogato is my safe port whenever I feel I'm sinking in a sea of admin, or when my energies have hit a historic low. It requires me to stop, take a breather, put the Moka pot on the stove, wait for the ice cream to soften (there always is a tub in the freezer for emergencies) and just enjoy the moment. It's the quickest form of physical and moral pick-me-up I know — sugar and caffeine delivered in seconds. And to think that affogato means 'drowned'... I have always seen it as more of a life jacket.

Mood aside, what it also saves is dessert, especially when time for dessert can't be found, or when dinner plans are made at the last minute. The fact that most people like its main components (coffee and ice cream) helps. It also helps that the word affogato often triggers sweet memories of holidays in sunny locations.

Unlike the version I inhale myself, which is usually pretty basic, the sort of affogato I whip up for guests is usually a bit richer in flavours and textures. A favourite take — a nod to the fondness most Venetians have for anything tasting vaguely of almonds — involves a splash of amaretto liqueur, a few crumbled amaretti biscuits and a big scoop of, well, almond gelato.

Place 4 ice cream cups or tumblers in the freezer for 20 minutes.

Next, take them out and pour in the amaretto liqueur. Scoop the ice cream on top, and then cover with crumbled amaretti.

Serve with the hot coffee poured on top at the very last minute.

Baked Peaches with Mascarpone Cream

SERVES 4

55g | ¼ cup unsalted butter, softened

55g | ¼ cup caster sugar

4 large white or yellow peaches, halved, stone removed

8 basil leaves, plus more to decorate (see Note below)

250g | 8¾oz mascarpone

30g | ¼ cup icing sugar

Note: A pinch of ground cinnamon or half a vanilla pod are both good replacements for basil. Dried lavender works a charm here, too. And if the fat content of mascarpone is a worry, swap it with whipped ricotta — a more than respectable substitute.

In my family we can't agree on what the ideal peach should be. One likes it crunchy, the other so ripe that it sprays juice all over his face. One prefers it white, another blushed, and another yellow. One hates the fuzzy skin and peels it off; the other bites into it without blinking.

There is one way with peaches, however, that settles all disputes, and it's when peaches are baked to melting tenderness. At that point, colour or skin type is not an issue any more; everybody digs in and scrapes every last drop of sugary syrup from the pan.

Served warm, basted with their own buttery juices, and freshened up by a handful of basil leaves, these peaches are good with anything creamy: ice cream, certainly, but also whipped, sweetened mascarpone, a recurrent ingredient in Venetian desserts since the golden age of the Serenissima.

———————

Preheat the oven to 180°C | 350°F | gas mark 4. In a small bowl, cream the butter and sugar until well combined. Wet the bottom of a baking tray with 30ml | 2 tablespoons of water and then arrange the peaches on top, skin-side down. Spoon the butter and sugar mixture in the holes left by the peach stones. Bake for 45 minutes, or until the peaches are very soft, then turn them and bake them for 5 more minutes with the cut side down.

Transfer the peaches to a plate and keep them warm in the turned-off oven. Pour the liquid left on the bottom of the tray into a pan and reduce over a medium-high heat for 5 minutes. Remove from the heat; add the basil leaves and toss. Leave to infuse for 10 minutes, then strain the liquid and keep it warm.

Prepare the mascarpone cream by whipping the mascarpone and icing sugar in a large bowl until fluffy and fully combined. Serve the peaches with a spoonful of basil-infused syrup and a dollop of mascarpone cream on top. Decorate with a few extra basil leaves if you like.

Raspberries with Rosé Wine

SERVES 4

300g | 10½oz raspberries

30g | 2 tablespoons caster
sugar

160ml | ⅔ cup rosé wine,
chilled

If there's still a little bit of wine left at the end of lunch (and this is true especially in the summer), my family like to slice some fruit into their glass, add more wine and call it dessert. Peaches and strawberries are excellent here, and a classic choice, but if given the chance, I'd always reach for the raspberries — particularly the tiny, flavour-bursting gems growing in the corner of my parents' garden.

Now, the perfect partner to raspberries, in my mind, is rosé. The colour pairing is irresistible, the alliteration too, not to mention that rosé and raspberries both share the same summery soul. Together, they create a sprightly fruity dessert of sorts that is grown-up yet vaguely childish — reminiscent of fruit salad — and keeps things light and fresh after a generous meal.

If raspberries are not your thing, or you want to stir things up a bit, substitute wild strawberries, chopped strawberries or sliced white peaches. For strawberries, I'd use sparkling Moscato Fior d'Arancio rather than rosé; an aromatic white wine will be divine with peaches.

Place the raspberries in a medium bowl. Add the sugar and wine and leave to macerate in the fridge for about 20 minutes, tossing a couple of times.

Spoon the raspberries into 4 dishes or glasses and serve topped with some of their soaking liquid.

To make this a more substantial dessert, spoon the macerated berries over vanilla ice cream or mascarpone cream (see page 231).

Polenta Olive Oil Cake with Rosemary & Lemon

For the cake:

240ml | 1 cup extra virgin
  olive oil, plus more for
  the tin

170g | heaped 1 cup fine
  polenta (such as Fioretto)

150g | 1½ cups ground
  almonds

1½ teaspoons baking powder

Finely grated zest of
  2 unwaxed lemons

3 teaspoons very finely
  chopped rosemary leaves

½ teaspoon fine-grain sea salt

5 eggs

225g | 1 cup caster sugar

For the syrup:

Juice of 2 lemons (about
  120ml | ½ cup), strained

110g | ½ cup caster sugar

Sprigs of rosemary and
  rosemary flowers, to
  decorate (optional)

Atop a tiny village in the Euganean Hills is a villa whose garden is dotted with precious pot-grown lemon trees. The plants, hardly typical in northern Italy, thrive in the warm microclimate of the hills, alongside olive trees and other Mediterranean species. In the right season, the fragrance of the zagare, *the citrus blossoms, is soporific; so is that of the fruits once they come to full maturity, their skin scarred and blemished but so pregnant with essential oils that one could dab it behind the ears instead of cologne. I had been indifferent to the charm of citrus fruits until my first visit to that garden: after, the scent of lemons became one of the things in life I can hardly do without.*

I love citrus in just about anything, and in cooking I like pairing it with herbs of the same origin — lemon and rosemary, orange and wild fennel and so on. This cake is an example of just such an aromatic marriage. The spark came on a rainy day in London, chatting about Italian food and sunny lands over a piece of excellent lemon rosemary cake with my friend Mehr. The cake ticked all boxes for me, so much so that I left the café motivated to recreate it at home.

The result is this recipe. Its body is that of a pound cake, made quintessentially Venetian by means of polenta flour and ground almonds, but kept deeply Mediterranean (or perhaps, Euganean) thanks to the olive oil, rosemary and lemon. The texture is moist and vaguely crunchy, the flavour grassy and zingy, fresh and resinous, sweet and slightly sour. It is the sort of cake you never get tired of, no matter how much you eat. You've been warned.

* This cake works well in a 23cm | 9-inch springform cake tin, too. Reduce the cooking time accordingly — check for doneness at 40 minutes.

Preheat the oven to 180°C | 350°F | gas mark 4. Brush a 900g (23cm | 9-inch) loaf tin* with olive oil and dust with a spoonful of polenta — shake to coat all sides.

In a medium bowl, combine the polenta, ground almonds, baking powder, lemon zest, rosemary leaves and salt. In a separate, larger bowl, beat the eggs with a hand-held electric whisk until frothy.

While still beating at a high speed, pour in the oil in a thin stream; you'll eventually see the two coming together into a smooth, frothy and perfectly emulsified mixture. Next, add the sugar and keep beating until incorporated. Finally, add the flour mixture in 3 batches, folding through at every addition. At this point, the batter should look smooth, but a bit granular and on the runny side.

Pour the batter into the prepared tin and level it. Transfer to the middle shelf of the oven and bake for 1 hour, or until a knife or skewer runs clean through the centre. (If, halfway through, you notice that the top is becoming too dark, cover with a piece of foil.)

Once done, remove from the heat and allow the cake to cool in the tin for about 30 minutes. Then, run a knife along the edges to unmould it and turn out onto a wire rack to cool completely. It might be that, although cooked all the way through, the cake will sink a little in the middle while cooling; this is fairly normal, and won't compromise the overall texture.

To make the syrup, heat the lemon juice in a small pan. As soon as you see it reaching the boil, add the sugar and stir until dissolved. Reduce the heat to a simmer and let the syrup thicken and reduce to about half its initial volume. Remove from the heat and let it cool for 5 minutes, then brush it all over the top of the cake. Leave to set for at least 1 hour before slicing. If you like, you can garnish the cake with sprigs of rosemary and rosemary flowers.

Sweet Potato Tart

For the pastry:

250g | 2 cups + 1 tablespoon
   plain flour, sifted, plus
   more for dusting

110g | 1 cup icing sugar

Finely grated zest of
   1 unwaxed lemon

125g | ½ cup + 1 tablespoon
   unsalted butter, chilled
   and cut into small cubes

1 egg plus 1 yolk, lightly
   beaten

For the filling:

700g | 1½lb white sweet
   potato (see Note overleaf)

1 teaspoon ground cinnamon

⅛ teaspoon freshly grated
   nutmeg

Pinch of fine-grain sea salt

Finely grated zest of
   1 unwaxed orange (optional)

50g | 3½ tablespoons
   caster sugar

2 eggs, lightly beaten

160ml | ⅔ cup whole milk

60ml | ¼ cup grappa (or
   use freshly squeezed and
   strained orange juice)

10g | 1½ tablespoons
   cornflour

Icing sugar and ground
   cinnamon, to dust
   (optional)

If you ever find yourself in a Venetian greengrocer some time in autumn, you might be lucky enough to stumble upon a variety of sweet potato marketed as 'Patate USA'. Despite the store's laughable attempt to shake off a bit of healthy provincialism by means of fancy words such as 'USA' (that's a fancy word in the countryside of Veneto, in case you're wondering), what you have actually found is a true niche product from the area, one to which Venetians are so nostalgically attached that they are able to sustain hour-long conversations about its qualities and merits. You've found patate americane.

Patate americane, *particularly those grown in Southern Veneto, are small in size, with a beige, sandy skin concealing a white, dense, smooth, sugary flesh whose low water and high sugar content mark their superiority over most yams. The variety became extremely popular in the area after it was brought over from the Americas and found a suitable habitat in the fertile flatlands of Polesine. Locals enjoy them simply roasted (best cooked under hot coals), and eat them as a warming snack, better still if accompanied by a glass of new wine. Another classic use is in gnocchi (large knots of sweet potato and flour, seasoned, Renaissance-style, with molasses, cinnamon and grated cheese) or in traditional baked goods.*

My family never made Renaissance gnocchi, but repurposed any leftover patate americane *in the form of* crostata *— a tart that is curiously reminiscent of American pumpkin pie. The shell is made of traditional Italian* pasta frolla *(sugar pastry). The filling, on the other hand, is original, devised by Mum and tweaked by me. Soft, creamy and custardy, it has a subtle sweetness enhanced by warm spices that makes it typically autumnal.*

CONTINUED OVERLEAF

Note: It might be hard to come across the specific sweet potato variety mentioned on the previous page. If you can't find it, use a purple-skinned, white-fleshed sweet potato instead. The only thing to bear in mind is that the filling should be creamy rather than loose. Strain the potato purée overnight if it looks too wet, then adjust the dose of cornflour to come to the desired thickness.

Preheat the oven to 180°C | 350°F | gas mark 4. Wash and pat dry the sweet potato. Cut it into 3–4 large chunks, wrap them in foil and roast until very tender, about 1 hour.

Meanwhile, make the pastry. Combine the flour, sugar and lemon zest in a large bowl. Rub the butter into the flour using the tips of your fingers until you have a coarse, crumbly mix. Add the egg and the yolk, and knead until the dough comes together into a smooth ball — try not to overwork it. Wrap it in cling film and leave to rest in the fridge for at least 30 minutes, or up to 1 hour.

Remove the sweet potato chunks from the oven and allow them to cool. Leave the oven on at the same temperature. Peel and mash the potatoes with a fork, masher or ricer. Add the mash to a large bowl along with all the other ingredients for the filling. Stir into a smooth, creamy batter. Set aside.

Roll the chilled pastry into a really thin circle that is large enough to cover a 26cm | 10-inch loose-bottomed tart tin. (Dust your work surface with flour and move/turn the dough often so it doesn't stick.) Flip the dough onto the tin using a rolling pin; press it with your fingertips so it sticks to the surface of the tin and cut off any excess. Pierce the surface all over with a fork, cover with parchment and top with baking beans (or real dried beans, which you can then re-use for this purpose). Blind bake for 10 minutes.

Remove the base from the oven and then remove the parchment and baking beans. Pour in the filling and level it. Return the now-filled tart to the oven and bake for 45 minutes, or until the filling is set and the edges of the crust are deeply golden. Remove from the oven and leave to cool completely. If you like, right before serving you can dust the *crostata* with icing sugar mixed with a generous pinch of ground cinnamon. The sugar will melt quickly due to the moist nature of the filling, but the cinnamon will leave a warm, spiced imprint that is very pleasant.

This tart is even better the second day as the filling has had the time to rest and set.

Ricotta Pudding Cake

SERVES 8

Unsalted butter, for the tin
100g | 1 cup ground almonds,
   plus more for the tin
300g | 10½oz fresh ricotta,
   drained
5 eggs
120g | heaped 1 cup icing
   sugar, sifted
30ml | 2 tablespoons orange
   blossom water

* Ricotta literally means
're-cooked' and is produced
by re-boiling the whey leftover
from the cheese-making
process. It can be made using
most kinds of whey — cow,
sheep, goat and buffalo are
all found in Italy.

Ricotta* might not be the first thing that comes to mind when discussing the food of Veneto. And yet, it has been part of the culinary heritage of the region for decades, featuring in all sorts of dishes, from gnocchi to cakes.

Venetians call ricotta puina. *Flipping through old recipe books written in dialect, I stumbled upon a few recipes for* torta de puina — *a cake made with little more than flour, ricotta and eggs. The idea intrigued me and triggered many trials (and many errors). I settled on a cake in which ricotta and eggs are the main ingredients, and give way to a temptingly tender number that sits somewhere between a crustless cheesecake and a flan. Orange blossom water is my elected aromatic element — in small amounts, it imparts the most pleasant floweriness.*

I love this cake for many reasons: for its simplicity, mostly, but also for its ability to welcome a few variations. Grappa-soaked raisins, candied citrus peel or roughly chopped dark chocolate all make nice additions. As for toppings, a dollop of orange-blossom whipped cream or a berry coulis are both fabulous ideas (as are flowers!).

Preheat the oven to 150°C | 300°F | gas mark 2 and liberally butter a 23cm | 9-inch springform cake tin or equivalent bundt, pudding or brioche mould. Dust the inside of the tin with ground almonds.

Press the drained ricotta through a fine-mesh sieve into a bowl to 'rice' it. In a separate bowl, whisk the eggs with the icing sugar until airy, light and pale yellow. Add the ground almonds, ricotta and orange blossom water and fold through gently to incorporate.

Pour the batter into the tin. Set it on the middle shelf of the oven and bake for about 1½ hours, or until swollen and golden on top and cooked through (insert a skewer in the middle to check; the exact time will depend on the depth of the mould/tin you are using).

Remove from the oven and allow to cool in the tin. Once at room temperature, carefully unmould onto a plate. Slice and serve.

Zabaglione with Muscat Wine

SERVES 4

4 egg yolks, at room
    temperature
55g | ¼ cup caster sugar
60ml | ¼ cup Moscato passito
    (see Note below)

Note: Moscato passito is a
type of non-sparkling Italian
dessert wine that is often aged
but, unlike port or sherry,
never fortified. It can be
substituted with other types
of passito wine from different
grape varieties or regions, or
with a French equivalent such
as Sauternes. Each wine will
impart its own unique flavour
to the zabaglione.

Our Venetian wedding took place just before Christmas, so our cake was a festive variation on the classic millefoglie, *with a thin slice of panettone substituting the central layer of puff pastry, and lots of marsala-infused zabaglione replacing the classic vanilla custard. The cake was excellent — not a crumb was left behind — but what made it even better was the dried-fruity, syrupy* passito *with which we paired it. Even in the oblivion of the moment — the party, the people, the fact I was married — the magic combination of creamy zabaglione and floral sweet wine remains one of the most vivid memories I have of that day. The idea for this* zabaione al moscato *sparked from there.*

Zabaglione has to be one of the most iconic Venetian puddings. It dates back to the golden era of the Serenissima, *when it was a luxury reserved to the few who could enjoy it cold, served in lacy Murano glass cups. Of the many variations out there — with white wine, rum, marsala or* malvasia; *with cinnamon, lemon or vanilla; with whipped cream or egg whites — I chose to follow a foolproof, easy-to-remember algorithm: one egg yolk, one tablespoon of sugar and one tablespoon of liqueur per person. This seemingly basic combination produces a velvety, rich and yet airy zabaglione. The added aroma of passito, for its part, is subtle but discernible — not unlike the scent left in the room when someone wearing cologne has just walked through.*

When served as a stand-alone dessert, zabaglione is often sent out with biscuits for dipping — Venetian baicoli, *but also* savoiardi (ladyfingers) *and amaretti (see page 227). A different way to serve it would be with apple cake (see page 125). I also like it on lightly toasted panettone, or with a still-warm* fritole *(see pages 123–124).*

CONTINUED OVERLEAF

VARIATION:

Substitute the wine for
4 tablespoons of
strong-brewed coffee, or
4 short shots of espresso.

Prepare the bain-marie. Choose a pan upon which a medium heatproof bowl can sit comfortably. Fill the pan with just enough water to almost reach the bottom of the bowl, without actually touching it. Place the pan of water over a medium heat.

Off the heat, use the bowl to whisk the egg yolks with the sugar until pale yellow and creamy. Add the wine and keep whisking until combined.

When the water is simmering, reduce the heat to low. Place the bowl on top and start whisking it gently but steadily, always in the same direction. All the while, ensure that the custard never boils; lift the bowl from the water and whisk quickly if you see it bubbling. Carry on until you have a dense, creamy texture, then place the bowl of zabaglione in cold water and whisk until it has cooled to room temperature.

Spoon the zabaglione into four serving cups and chill in the fridge until set. Alternatively, pour it into a serving dish. Serve with cake, or any of the suggestions on the previous page.

Lemon Sorbet with Prosecco & Grappa

SERVES 4

400g | 14oz lemon sorbet
30ml | 2 tablespoons
  grappa, chilled
60ml | ¼ cup prosecco, chilled

It seemed appropriate to close this section with a glass of refreshing, digestive sgroppino. *In Veneto, it's the drink that signals the end of a hearty meal, the sort of drink that could help digest rocks, or at least a generous portion of* baccalà *or the twenty courses of a wedding reception. Its powers are nothing short of miraculous.*

This is my version of sgroppino. *Feel free to use vodka or limoncello instead of grappa. Other possible variations include green apple or peach sorbet in place of lemon.*

Combine all the ingredients in a blender and blend until smooth. Pour into 4 chilled champagne glasses and serve immediately.

In this last section you'll find a handful of beloved recipes for sweet and savoury preserves, spread across the four seasons but leaning heavily towards spring and summer. Some are preparations we made regularly at home; others, like dried figs, have been created with specific Venetian storecupboard staples in mind; others again, I had the luck to encounter, taste, love and acquire the recipes for on my journey, so that I could recreate them in my own kitchen. You'll discover more about them as you go, but for now, I'd suggest you stock up on jars.

PART III
Pantry

Preserving the Seasons

I once read a definition of preserving that resonates with me: in a way, it is a hymn against waste as much as a celebration of bounty. It's a description that rang true for a variety of reasons.

My husband laughs at me for reserving any scraps of food, no matter how meagre — for saving carrot greens and fennel fronds from the threat of the compost bin, and for being resolute about finding a place for leftovers in the following meals. It can drive people crazy, but this sometimes eye-rolling thriftiness is a result of what I've been exposed to: I have never seen anyone in my family throwing food away — not a piece of dry bread, not a tomato, not a fig, not a pizza crust, nothing. There always seemed to be a better place for it. Venetians, like most Italians, had to learn to be inventive, resourceful cooks — something that becomes evident not just in the way leftovers are often repurposed according to traditional *ricette di recupero*, but also in the manner in which abundance is often dealt with: through a policy of saving and preserving. It's a 'waste not, want not' attitude that I observed and absorbed at an early age, and that has stuck with me ever since.

I have mentioned at points in this book that my grandparents used to have their own vegetable gardens and fruit trees (cherries, plums, figs, pomegranates), and that they would grow bundles of produce for us to enjoy. What I didn't mention is that they produced so much, especially in the summer, that they were often left with no alternative but to pull up their sleeves and get canning, pickling and jamming. They had good reasons to do so: it wasn't just about not wasting for the sake of it, rather it was about taking pride in what they produced, and, perhaps more importantly, about a mindset that encouraged you to be well stocked against the prospect of winter, like *The Ant and the Grasshopper*. Although we are now far from times of necessity, preserving is seeing a revival. As books on the subject flourish, a new generation of home preservers is taking on the time-honoured habit — a clear sign, this, that there's room for a 'waste not, want not' philosophy in our modern lives.

BEFORE YOU START: SOME ADVICE ON PRESERVING FOOD IN JARS

Preserving is a wonderful practice, but it requires some foresight and care to ensure that the food we put in jars won't spoil and is safe to eat. The first step is to work in a clean environment and use the right equipment. I tend to only use jars (new or recycled, as long as they are not chipped) for which I can purchase new, screw-on lids every time. This is because the rubber on the underside of the lid (essential to create the seal) is only reliable once.

When setting up for a preserving session, the first thing to do is to sterilise the equipment. Begin with washing jars and lids in plenty of hot soapy water. Rinse thoroughly to remove any trace of washing-up liquid, which might spoil the flavour of your preserve, and dry them on a clean tea towel. Next, set the jars in a warm oven (around 120°C | 250°F | gas mark ½) for 30 minutes. This serves three purposes: it sterilises the jars, dries them and keeps them warm. Ensure that the jars are hot when filling them. The lids don't need to go in the oven for long. Leave them only for a couple of minutes, just enough to warm them up, right before using.

Then, when in the process of filling your jars (a large-mouth funnel might help in some cases), make sure to leave a gap about 5mm | ¼ inch from the rim and wipe the jar clean with kitchen paper to get rid of any residue that would compromise the sealing. Finally, close tightly but without forcing, so as not to ruin the rubber underneath the lid.

After being jarred, some types of preserves (low-acidity sauces such as passata, or certain pickles; I will specify which in the actual recipe instructions) are best processed through a water-bath canning in order to be shelf-stable and extra safe. To do that, I rely on a large, tall stockpot in which the jars can sit comfortably and be completely submerged. The process begins with placing the filled, closed jars into the stockpot. To keep jars in place and avoid breakage, you can use a fitted rack or (and this is Grandma's trick) tea towels: wrap one or two around the jars and they won't clash against each other. Next, fill the pot with cold water, ensuring that the jars are covered by 5–6cm | 2–2½ inches. Close the pot with a lid and bring everything to the boil. Boil the jars for about 20 minutes (the exact time will depend on the size of the jars), then turn off the heat and leave them to cool in the water for 10 minutes. At this point, lift them from the water (try not to touch the lid but rather the jar, as the inside of the lid is still malleable and any stress might compromise the sealing process; a jar lifter helps with this) and set them on a clean tea towel to cool. After a while, you should hear the pinging of lids sealing. After 24 hours, check that the centre of the lid is concave and that the lid itself holds on tight. Now, wash the jars again to get rid of any residue. Pat them dry and store them in a cool dry place. If by any chance a jar hasn't sealed properly, store it in the fridge and eat its contents first.

ASPARAGI BIANCHI SOTT'OLIO
White Asparagus in Oil

SUGO DI POMODORO
Tomato Sauce with Basil & Garlic

GIARDINIERA
Pickled Vegetable Medley

PEPERONI IN VASETTO
Preserved Peppers, Two Ways

CIPOLLINE SOTT'ACETO
Pickled Baby Onions

CILIEGIE ALLA GRAPPA
Grappa-Soaked Cherries

PESCHE SCIROPPATE
Peaches in Syrup

MARMELLATA DI FICHI VERDI E VANIGLIA
Green Fig Vanilla Jam

FICHI SECCHI
Dried Figs

PERSEGADA O COTOGNATA
Candied Quince Paste

White Asparagus in Oil

MAKES 6 × 250ML | ½-PINT JARS

2kg | 4lb 6oz white asparagus

480ml | 2 cups white wine
   vinegar

12 bay leaves

4 juniper berries

5g | 1 teaspoon fine-grain
   sea salt

3g | 1 teaspoon black
   peppercorns

Extra virgin olive oil

VARIATION:

You can apply a similar
procedure to baby or small
violet artichokes, cleaned
and quartered.

The storecupboard in our shared kitchen in Padua was always filled with jars of preserved white asparagus. They were a gift from Paolo's mum, Agnese, a generous soul and wonderful cook. Agnese lives in Bassano, land of the best white asparagus, which she'd buy by the box to preserve in oil as soon as they came into season. She'd give some to her son.

Unsurprisingly, Paolo was very jealous of his asparagus jars, but he still shared them with us. And I'm glad he did, for those asparagus saved dinner on more than one night: a piece of Asiago cheese and a morsel of bread and I was in my happy place.

My take on Agnese's recipe is part winging, part flavour memory and part Paolo's suggestions. The outcome is a lush oil pickle spiked by the spiced note of black peppercorns and the aroma of juniper. Reduce the amounts of both for a more neutral flavour.

Trim the bottom of the asparagus stalks so that they are pretty much the same length. Rinse them quickly under cold running water; pat them dry. Peel off any stringy, woody parts using a vegetable peeler; cut the stems into halves and then into batons. (Reserve the tips for a risotto or sauté them in butter and eat with scrambled eggs.)

Bring 480ml | 2 cups water and the vinegar to the boil with 6 of the bay leaves, the juniper berries and salt. Reduce to a simmer and blanch the asparagus for about 3 minutes. Drain and transfer to a tea towel to dry.

Sterilise 6 × 250ml | ½-pint jars and screw-on lids (see page 251). Fill them with asparagus, packing them tightly while leaving 1cm | ½ inch from the rim. In each jar, fit a bay leaf and a couple of peppercorns. Cover with olive oil. Tap gently to free air bubbles, and top up with more oil if the level drops below 5mm | ¼ inch from the rim. Close tightly with dry, sterilised lids.

Leave to mature at room temperature for 1 week. Store the jars in a cool place (or, better still, in the fridge) for up to 6 months.

Tomato Sauce with Basil & Garlic

MAKES 6 × 500ML | 1-PINT JARS

5kg | 11lb saucing tomatoes
(see recipe introduction)
6 garlic cloves, whole but
lightly crushed
Small bunch of basil
Extra virgin olive oil
Fine-grain sea salt, to taste

Note: Once open, a jar of sauce
can serve many purposes.
Use it whenever tomato sauce
is called for — in braises,
stews and for pasta. For the
simplest *pasta al pomodoro*, for
example, all you need to do is
warm up the sauce, toss the
pasta in it, and add a generous
glug of olive oil and a light
snowfall of grated Parmesan.
Done.

Summers in Veneto are hot and humid. They are hard to bear, though they generally grant the gifted grower a hefty harvest of whatever they're nurturing. In my family, we are good at growing tomatoes, and this talent leads to intense tomato canning sessions throughout the entire tomato season.

Hunched over the food mill, sweat coating her forehead, Grandma would mash crates of tomatoes without rest. A barricade of mismatched jars in front of her, she would fill them to the brim, ease a piece of garlic and a leaf of basil on top and close them tight. A bashed aluminium pot with water would be boiling all the while, ready to welcome the legion of jars for a last bath and the final pop that would seal them for good. They would then make their final journey to the dim, cool cellar, lining the storage shelves alongside other jars of kindred spirit.

Making tomato sauce is relaxing, pleasurable and fulfilling. It's messy, hot and lengthy, too, but it gives results that are there to last for a good season or two. All that's needed to get down to it, aside from a host of ripe tomatoes, is the right equipment. In Italy, no tomato canning takes place without a food mill (or mouli). I encourage you to find one, it's the sort of small investment that will last a lifetime (and that can be used for making smooth vegetable purées and silky jams, too).

The best tomato varieties to make sauce with are the San Marzano, the Costoluto and the Riccio. Whether a tomato is good for making sauce is easy to find out: good ones will lose their shape very quickly, releasing their juices and giving way to a smooth, velvety sauce, which can then be milled into an even glossier passata. In some households, a battuto *of finely chopped celery, carrot and onion is used as a base for sauce. Grandma, however, prefers cooking her tomatoes without much of anything, adding garlic for character and basil for freshness at the very end.*

Wash the tomatoes thoroughly and place them in a bucket or large basin. Cut them in half and remove and discard the seeds. Place the tomato halves in the largest stockpot you have — or divide them between 2.

Heat the pot(s) over a medium-low heat. At one point, you will see that the tomatoes are starting to release their juices. Add a splash of water (about 60ml | ¼ cup) and leave them to bubble down, stirring occasionally to make sure they cook evenly. Once they have let out all their liquid, reduce the heat to its minimum and allow the sauce to simmer for about 1 hour. Check and stir it often.

Meanwhile, sterilise 6 × 500ml | 1-pint jars and screw-on lids (see page 251). Go back to your sauce and taste it; season with a generous dash of salt (how much depends on your personal preference; start with about 8g | 1½ teaspoons fine-grain sea salt), stir, wait a couple of minutes, then taste again and season some more if needed. Remove from the heat and allow the sauce to cool ever so slightly so that you can handle it comfortably. Working in batches, scoop the tomatoes and pass them through the mill secured over a bowl small enough for it to sit comfortably (as soon as the bowl fills up, transfer the sauce to another container and carry on). Once in a while, discard the scraps, peels, seeds and fibrous bits to make room for more tomatoes. For an extra-smooth sauce, you can mill it twice; I'm usually happy with one milling.

Fill the hot sterilised jars with the sauce, leaving 1cm | ½ inch at the top. Place a garlic clove and 2 basil leaves on top, then finish with 1 tablespoon of oil. Close tightly with dry, sterilised lids. Proceed with the water bath canning (see page 251).

Store the sealed jars in a cool, dry place for up to 6 months. Keep any open (or unsealed) jars in the fridge and consume within 2 weeks.

GIARDINIERA
Pickled Vegetable Medley

MAKES 4 × 1-LITRE |
1-QUART JARS

1.5 litres | 6¼ cup white
  wine vinegar

1.5 litres | 6¼ cup water

30g | 2 tablespoons
  caster sugar

30g | 2 tablespoons fine-grain
  sea salt

2 bay leaves

3g | 1 teaspoon black
  peppercorns

4 juniper berries

1 red chilli

300g | 10½oz carrots, peeled
  and julienned

300g | 10½oz red pepper,
  deseeded and cut into
  thin strips

300g | 10½oz green or yellow
  pepper, deseeded and cut
  into thin strips

600g | 1lb 5oz cauliflower
  florets

300g | 10½oz celery, trimmed
  and cut into thin strips

300g | 10½oz baby onions,
  quartered

300g | 10½oz cucumber,
  cut into thin strips

300g | 10½oz green beans,
  trimmed and halved

Giardiniera is a mix of crisp, seasonal vegetables pickled in a slightly sweet, piquant liquid, and commonly used in the very 1990s preparation that is rice salad (see page 171). It's not unusual to see it served as an appetiser, either on its own or alongside cold cuts and aged cheese. Although giardiniera is very to find in stores, the advantages of making it at home are multiple, not least the fact that it's a great way to use up large amounts of seasonal vegetables, and that it's easily customised according to taste.

The combination I've listed here, for instance, is a classic summer mix, but I like to change it frequently, based on what I find at the market. Other vegetables that work, depending on the season, are asparagus, romanesco, radishes, beetroot, shallots, broccoli, parsnip and celeriac. Experiment to find the flavour and colour mixes that suit your tastes.

Place the vinegar, water, sugar and salt in a large pan. When boiling, add the bay leaves, peppercorns, juniper and chilli, and allow them to infuse the simmering liquid for about 5 minutes. Now, blanch the vegetables in the liquid (through a chinois, if you wish), 1 variety at a time, and strain them while they are still fairly crunchy (onions and cauliflower florets will take about 3–4 minutes, the rest about 2 minutes), setting them on clean tea towels or kitchen paper to dry.

When all the vegetables have been blanched, strain the cooking liquid and discard the aromatics. Fill 4 × 1-litre | 1-quart sterilised jars (see page 251) with a mix of the blanched vegetables, leaving about 2cm | ¾ inch from the rim. Cover with the strained vinegar mixture (you might have some picking liquid leftover depending on how much evaporates during simmering) and press down the vegetables with the back of a wooden spoon to ensure that there are no air bubbles and that the vegetables are completely submerged, leaving about 5mm | ¼ inch between the liquid and the rim. Close tightly with dry, sterilised lids.

Store your *giardiniera* in a cool dry place for up to 3 months, and any open jars in the fridge.

Preserved Peppers, Two Ways

My husband has a soft spot for any preserve featuring a medley of red and yellow peppers. He discovered their existence upon his first visit to Veneto. Of all the possible variants available in store, two captured him in particular: a sweet and sour pickle and an oil-based number with charred strips of peppers bobbing in it. The next step was trying to reproduce them both at home — a task made easy once we moved to Bra, in Piedmont, and had access to the wonderful (abundant, cheap!) peppers grown in the area.

Unable to choose one version over the other, I include them both here. The pickled peppers are delicious in salads or as an antipasto. The charred ones are fantastic in a sandwich with a piece of chicken breast or some aged cheese, or stuffed with an anchovy and a caper and rolled up into moreish morsels.

VERSION 1: IN AGRODOLCE *Sweet & Sour Pickle*

MAKES 4 × 250ML | ½-PINT JARS

1.2kg | 2lb 10oz red and
  yellow peppers
800ml | 3⅓ cups white
  wine vinegar
90g | scant ½ cup
  granulated sugar
30g | 2 tablespoons fine-grain
  sea salt

Rinse the peppers and pat them dry. Remove the stem, seeds and pith. Cut them into thin strips and set aside.

Bring the vinegar, sugar and salt to the boil in a large pan. Add the pepper strips and cook for 10 minutes, until tender but still crunchy. Lift out with a slotted spoon and transfer to a plate; reserve the liquid and leave both to cool.

Meanwhile, sterilise 4 × 250ml | ½-pint jars and screw-on lids (see page 251). Once ready, pack the still-hot jars with peppers, leaving about 1cm from the top. Cover with the reserved liquid. Press the peppers down with a wooden spoon to get rid of any air bubbles and top up with more liquid if needed, ensuring that the vegetables are completely submerged and that there is only 5mm | ¼ inch between the fill level and the rim.

Close tightly with dry, sterilised lids. Leave to mature for at least 1 week. Store in a cool place (or in the fridge) for up to 3 months, and keep in the fridge once opened.

VERSION 2: GRIGLIATI SOTT'OLIO *Grilled & Packed in Oil*

1.5kg | 3lb 5oz red and
  yellow peppers
4 garlic cloves, sliced
4 sprigs of thyme or marjoram
Extra virgin olive oil
  (200–300ml | ¾–1¼ cups)
Fine-grain sea salt, to taste

Sterilise 4 × 250ml | ½-pint jars and screw-on lids (see page 251). Wash the peppers and pat them dry. Place a griddle over a medium-high heat and char the peppers on all sides, until the skin is very blackened and the flesh feels tender all over.

Remove the peppers from the heat and leave to cool, then peel them and discard the stem, seeds and pith. Tear into strips and season them with a generous pinch of salt.

Pack the pepper strips into the sterilised jars, alternating them with the sliced garlic, leaving 2cm | ¾ inch from the top. Finish with a sprig of thyme or marjoram and cover with oil, pressing the peppers down with a wooden spoon to get rid of any air bubbles, and ensuring that the vegetables are completely submerged and there is only 5mm | ¼ inch between the fill level and the rim.

Close tightly with dry, sterilised lids. Leave to mature for at least 1 week. Store in a cool place (or in the fridge) for up to 6 months, and keep in the fridge once opened.

CIPOLLINE SOTT'ACETO
Pickled Baby Onions

MAKES 4 × 500ML | 1-PINT JARS

500g | 1lb 2oz fine-grain
   sea salt
2kg | 4lb 6oz baby onions
   (see Note below), peeled

For the pickling liquid:
1.3 litres | 5½ cups white
   wine vinegar
8 bay leaves
10g | 1 tablespoon
   peppercorns
30g | 2 tablespoons fine-grain
   sea salt
400g | 2 cups granulated
   sugar

Note: Borettane onions from
Emilia Romagna are an
excellent baby variety, ideal
for pickling. In Veneto you
can find them peeled and
ready to use, which saves
a few tears in the process.
Nevertheless, I find that the
peeling can be somewhat
therapeutic, if a bit fiddly.

Mariù Salvatori de Zuliani's A Tola Coi Nostri Veci *is one of the first cookbooks I ever owned. It's a recipe book entirely in Venetian dialect, and the fact that not many people could access its content has always been an incentive to cook from it, and to share the outcome on my blog. To date, the book remains one of the most complete sources on Venetian food ever published.*

This recipe for pickled baby onions has been adapted from one of Mariù's recipes. The onions are excellent eaten straight from the jar, or served alongside cheese and cured meats (see page 34).

Bring 4 litres | 16½ cups of water to the boil. Add the salt, stir to dissolve, then remove from the heat and leave to cool to room temperature. Place the peeled baby onions in a large bowl and cover with the cooled salted water. Leave to rest in the fridge for 24 hours.

The following day, drain the onions and rinse them thoroughly under cold running water. Arrange them on a clean tea towel and leave them to dry. Meanwhile, sterilise 4 × 500ml | 1-pint jars and screw-on lids (see page 251).

Prepare the pickling liquid by bringing the vinegar to the boil together with 4 of the bay leaves plus the peppercorns and salt. Once boiling, stir in the sugar. Simmer for 10 minutes, then remove from the heat and filter through a fine-mesh sieve to strain out the peppercorns and bay leaves.

Pack the still-hot jars with onions, leaving 2cm | ¾ inch clear at the top — gently pat the jars so the onions fall into place. Stick a new bay leaf in each jar then pour in the hot picking liquid, ensuring it covers the onions by about 1.5cm | ½ inch. Tap the jars gently to remove air bubbles and top up with more liquid if it drops below 5mm | ¼ inch from the rim. Close with sterilized lids and proceed with the water bath canning (see page 251).

Leave to mature for at least 3 weeks in a cool, dry place. Store for up to 6 months, and keep in the fridge once opened.

Grappa-Soaked Cherries

MAKES 3 × 500ML | 1-PINT JARS

800g | 1lb 12oz cherries
250g | 1¼ cup granulated
     sugar
Grappa (40–45% alcohol)
3 cinnamon sticks
6 cloves

* Veneto has a time-honoured
and flourishing cherry
production. The town of
Marostica, near Vicenza, is
especially renowned for its
excellent cherries, which bear
the IGP seal, as well as for its
yearly competition aimed at
crowning the best cherry
variety in the country.

The big cherry tree in Grandma's garden produced fruits that were unlike any other we could find at the market. Small, scarlet, sweet-with-a-slight-sourness, they were excellent in any form — straight from the fruit bowl, in cakes and drowned in liqueur. Indeed the cherries bobbing in jars in the pantry — drunk, spirited — were always 'our cherries': no one would have ever dared drowning plump and prized duroni *or* ciliegie di Marostica* *in alcohol. Those were reserved for eating only.*

Preserving cherries in alcohol is hardly a novelty, nor is it exclusive to Veneto. But it is an idea we have been implementing for a while, using grappa as the liqueur of choice. When the fruits are left to bathe in it for a while they create a cherry-flavoured spirit that is delightful sipped at the end of a meal, better still after a bowl of cherry-rippled ice cream.

The aromatics I list here are just a suggestion: vanilla works well, too, as does orange or lemon zest. And if cherries are not easy to come across where you are, try tiny plums such as mirabelles or damsons. As for the kind of grappa, opt for a neutral-flavoured sort; the cherries will impart plenty of flavour to it. And if grappa isn't your thing, dry gin is a good (if only more aromatic) alternative.

Wash the cherries very thoroughly and pat them dry. Trim the stems but leave a small portion intact and still attached to the fruit.

Fill 3 × 500ml | 1-pint jars (ensure that they are thoroughly clean and dry) with layers of cherries alternated with layers of sugar, making sure that the fruits are tightly packed but leaving about 2cm | ¾ inch clear from the rim.

Place 1 cinnamon stick and 2 cloves in each jar and top with grappa until the fruits are completely covered. Close tightly with new, clean, dry lids and leave to mature somewhere cool and preferably dark for at least 2 months (or, even better, 6). During the first 2 weeks, shake the contents regularly to ensure that the sugar doesn't deposit at the bottom. Consume within 1 year.

Peaches in Syrup

MAKES 4 × 500ML | 1-PINT JARS

3kg | 6½lb white or yellow
   peaches (or a mix), washed
1.5 litres | 6¼ cups water
600g | 2⅔ cups caster sugar
Zest of 2 unwaxed lemons,
   stripped with a vegetable
   peeler

Note: These are wonderful
served as they are, on yogurt
for breakfast with a bit of
their syrup, cut into a fruit
salad, or sliced on top of ice
cream. They can also be baked
into cakes or puréed to make a
Bellini of sorts.

Peaches and pears are the two fruits that Venetians like to preserve in simple syrup. The best of both kinds share a similar creamy texture that is particularly suited to being drowned in a sugary spirit.

When I plan to can peaches, I buy a whole crate of slightly firm fruits at the market and then leave them to ripen in a corner of the house until supple but not too squishy, and just ripe enough to fill the air with their unique perfume.

Sterilise 4 × 500ml | 1-pint jars (see page 251) and screw-on lids.

Bring a large pan of water to the boil. Add the peaches and blanch for about 5 minutes, turning them so that all sides have been in contact with the hot water. Remove them from the heat and, once slightly cooled, slide off the skins. Cut them in half and remove the stone and any stringy bits at the core. Set aside.

Bring the measured water to the boil. Stir in the sugar and strips of lemon zest and simmer for 2–3 minutes, until the sugar is dissolved. Discard the lemon strips; keep the liquid simmering over a low flame until ready to use.

Fill the still-hot sterilised jars with peach halves, leaving about 1cm | ½ inch clear from the rim. Pour over the hot syrup and then gently press the peaches down to get rid of any air bubbles. Top up with more syrup if needed to submerge the peaches completely, leaving 5mm | ¼ inch between liquid and rim.

Close the jars tightly with dry, sterilised lids. Store in a cool and dry place for up to 6 months and in the fridge after opening.

Green Fig Vanilla Jam

MAKES 7–8 × 250ML |
½-PINT JARS

2kg | 4lb 6oz green figs,
    peeled and roughly chopped
    (see Note overleaf)
½ vanilla pod
Juice of 1 lemon, strained
1kg | 5 cups granulated
    brown sugar (such as
    Demerara)

Fig trees are a common sight in Veneto. They break the flat line of the countryside, dot fields and line ditches, and bless people's gardens with their shade and abundant fruits. Most people pick and eat them as they are, in all their sugary, jammy goodness; a small number of people also make jam.

The habit of making jam never picked up in my family. It took an outsider's perspective to finally turn the figs growing on our many trees into jam. When Tracey moved to Veneto from England, she was genuinely amazed at the abundance of fruits at her disposal. Making jam came very instinctively to her; at no point did she accept that leaving fruits to fall to the ground was a sensible idea, definitely not with good figs.

Unlike many store-bought jams, Tracey's has a deep, caramel-like flavour from the unrefined brown sugar, a lovely perfume from the vanilla and a crunchy texture from the unstrained seeds. It has a loose feel, too, due to the relatively low sugar content; it runs down the edges of a slice of bread like a small avalanche — a lovely sight. Being low in sugar, it doesn't keep quite as long as normal jam, but this is hardly a problem given how good it is.

Before you begin, place a small saucer in the freezer: you'll need it later on to test the set (wrinkle test). Sterilise 8 × 250ml | ½-pint jars and screw-on lids (see page 251).

Place the figs together with the seeds of the vanilla pod, the pod itself and the lemon juice in a large pan. Set over a low heat and cook for about 20 minutes, stirring every now and then to prevent the fruit sticking to the bottom of the pan.

CONTINUED OVERLEAF

Note: Opt for figs that are unblemished and ripe but still supple. Green figs have an intense sweetness, which can be found in black figs from Provence, too: note that the colour of the jam will change depending on the type of figs you use. To help with the set, Tracey uses lemon juice. Aside from being a source of pectin, this imparts a much-needed hint of acidity that brightens and freshens the overall flavour of the jam.

Next, add the sugar and stir to help it dissolve. Bring to the boil and cook, stirring occasionally and skimming any scum, until the jam appears dense and glossy and the furious bubbling has receded a bit. To test it and see if it's set, either use a jam thermometer and check that the temperature has reached 105°C | 221° F, or do the wrinkle test. For the wrinkle test, remove the pot from the heat momentarily; take the saucer out of the freezer and spoon a bit of jam on top, then place it in the fridge for a couple of minutes, then take it out again and push the jam with a finger: if it wrinkles and doesn't flood back immediately, it's ready.

Take the still-hot sterilised jars and lids and set them over a clean tea towel. Fill them to the top with jam using a wide mouth funnel or a large spoon; you can discard the vanilla pod or add it to one of the jars. Note that both jars and jam should be very hot at this point.

Clean the rims with damp kitchen paper if there's any spillage. Screw the lids on tightly and turn the jars upside down for 30 minutes, then turn them right side up again. Leave them for a couple of hours so that they can cool and seal themselves. Store the sealed jars in a cool dry place for up to 6 months. Keep any unsealed or open jars in the fridge and consume within 2 weeks.

Dried Figs

Fresh figs, as many as you like
Fresh bay leaves, for storing

Dad is the one in our family who has the strongest feelings when it comes to dried figs. On the one hand, they remind him of his youth (a period of his life he is nostalgically attached to, despite the remarkable lack of comforts); on the other, he can't help but feeling mildly repelled by their sight, a clear sign that he ate more than he wishes to admit.

In the rural flatlands of southern Veneto, dried figs used to be the food of the poor. People who had no access to any source of protein in their diet — the seasonal salaried field workers, for example — used to eat dried figs with polenta at almost every meal, the former adding some fast-releasing sugar to fuel their demanding physical labour, the latter being the canonical hunger-soother. Whenever he was called to help in the fields, weeding or harvesting grapes, Dad, too, would fill his pockets with dried figs: they made any hard work more tolerable, he said. He was also often served bread and dried figs for breakfast, quickly warmed up in a pan with some lard or oil to soften them.

A recurrent ingredient in traditional cakes and sweet breads (see the pinza *on page 120), dried figs were always present in people's cupboards. However, despite the abundance of fresh figs available in the countryside, no one really dried them in-house; locals just bought them from the itinerant grocer and kept the fresh figs for eating, well, fresh. The habit of drying figs at home began with me, as a sort of tribute to this regional iconic food. Dad thinks I'm a bit nuts, but I've seen him eating my figs like he'll never do with any store-bought version, and I take that as a good sign.*

A sensible way to go about drying figs is to follow the example of the people living in the South of Italy — laying them on a wooden board and leaving them in the sun for a series of sweltering-hot late summer days, until the fruits have lost all their moisture and have concentrated their sugars. If this is not possible — perhaps because the sun of Puglia doesn't grace all places — the oven remains a good, reliable bet.

CONTINUED OVERLEAF

Note: Making dried figs at home might seem silly, not least because they are so easy to buy in stores. It is, however, a highly satisfying process, and a good alternative to jam (see pages 271–73) in the event that you do happen to lay your hands on lots of fresh figs, or own a prolific fig tree. The bay leaves impart a lovely, slightly aromatic note when left to rest for a couple of days, and a unique character that few store-bought alternatives have.

Preheat the oven, ideally with the fan on, to its lowest setting (50°C | 120°F). Wash the figs and check that they have no scars, bruises or traces of mould. Place them on a baking tray covered with parchment, stalk side up, and press them down gently to flatten them.

Roast the figs for about 8 hours (turn them every 30 minutes during this time so they dry evenly), or until they look deflated and wrinkly, and dark brown in colour. Allow them to cool inside the turned-off, open oven.

Once at room temperature, store the figs in a wooden box, a metal tin lined with parchment or a glass jar, alternating a layer of figs with a layer of bay leaves. Stored this way, in a closed container set in a cool dry place, they will keep for 4–6 weeks. You can also store them in an airtight container in the fridge.

Candied Quince Paste

SERVES 8–10

1kg | 2lb 3oz (about
  3 medium) quinces
450g | 1lb | 2 cups caster
  sugar, plus more as needed
Juice of 1 lemon, strained
Granulated sugar, for coating
Fresh bay leaves, for storing

Note: If you wish to serve
some of the jelly with cheese,
skip the final sugar rolling
and store the jelly in the fridge
as it is, in a glass jar; consume
within a month or so.

Traditionally a confectionery for St Martin's Day, on 11 November, the cotognata *sold in pastry shops and town fairs was set in small round moulds, imprinting decorative motifs on the surface of the jelly. The home version, in contrast, was moulded in square pans, cut and stored in tin boxes between layers of fresh aromatic bay leaves.*

––––––––––

Place the whole quinces in a large pan and cover with cold water. Set over a medium heat and cook for about 1 hour, or until they are very tender and the skin starts to come off. Drain and allow them to cool until manageable, then peel and cut them into chunks, discarding the core. Pass the chunks through a fine-mesh sieve to obtain a smooth purée. Alternatively, mash using a food mill and discard the scraps.

Weigh the purée, then transfer to a large heavy-based pan and mix it with equal amounts of caster sugar. (I tend to obtain about 450g | 1lb purée from 1kg of quince, so I have specified 450g | 1lb | 2 cups caster sugar here.) Add the strained lemon juice and stir to combine. Cover with a clean tea towel and leave the mix to sit for about 1 hour.

Next, put the pan over a low heat. Cook the quince paste for about 1½ hours from when it starts bubbling, stirring often. You'll hear the paste hissing first, then see it turn tawny, and eventually become very dense. When it looks thick and sticky, and detaches from the edges, it's done.

Tumble the hot paste into a 23cm | 9-inch square or round baking tin lined with cling film, spreading it to 2cm | ¾ inch thick. Allow it to cool completely, then leave to set in a cool dry place for about 24 hours, with a piece of parchment on top.

Once completely cooled and set, unmould the quince jelly and cut it into small squares. At this point, roll the squares in granulated sugar to make jelly candies. Store them in layers (preferably in a metal tin), separating each layer with a sheet of parchment and some fresh bay leaves. Keep in a cool, dry place (or better still, in an airtight container in the fridge) for up to 1 month.

ACKNOWLEDGEMENTS

Working on this book was a pleasure and a privilege, in part because of the generous people who helped me bring it to life. I am grateful and obliged to many.

Jesse, nothing could have ever happened without your unconditional support, patience and help. Thank you for loving my home region as if it were your own. This book is dedicated to you.

THANK YOU TO:

Mum and Dad, for passing down your love of food, and for allowing me to invade your kitchen with my cooking and crockery. Your encouragement means everything.

Grandma, for teaching me all you know about cooking. You're the soul of this book. Franca, for your kindness and wonderful produce. I'm forever indebted. Edo and Silvia, the best people to have around a table. Tracey, Renato, you're an inspiration.

Jon Elek, my agent, for believing in me. Millie Hopkins, for your diligence through the entire process.

Everyone at Faber: Sophie, John, Jack, you have been a joy to work with. Laura Hassan, for taking this project on board, and for your enthusiasm from day one.

Katherine Ailes, my editor: your support and guidance have been invaluable. Thank you for always hearing me out. Anna Green, my designer: you made this book so beautiful!

Emiko Davies, Rachel Roddy, Mehrunnisa Yusuf, Sophie Missing, Valentina Solfrini, Zaira Zarotti, Sabrina Ghayour, Sarah Roberts, Olia Hercules, Luisa Brimble for your inspiration, advice and for sharing your knowledge so generously. Vanessa Miles, for being my best cheerleader: your help was priceless. Lisa Fischoff, Jennifer Pitzer, Camilla Ferraro, for helping with recipe testing.

Paolo Toniolo and Roberta Signorini, for your friendship. You made our shared kitchen a wonderful place.

INDEX

Affettati Misti, 32–33, 34–35
Affogato al Caffè e Amaretto, 228, *229*
almonds
almond polenta shortbread tart, *118*, 119
ice cream 'drowned' in coffee & amaretto, 228, *229*
polenta cake with dried fruit, 120, *121*
polenta olive oil cake with rosemary & lemon, 234–35, *236*
ricotta pudding cake, 241, *242*, *243*
scallop gratin with almonds & orange, *152*, 153
soft bitter almond biscuits, *224–25*, *226*, 227
Amaretti Morbidi, *224–25*, *226*, 227
amaretto: ice cream 'drowned' in coffee &, 228, *229*
anchovies
bigoli with anchovies & onions, *66*, 67
hard-boiled eggs with, 142, *143*
mixed fried fish, *82*, 83
apples
radicchio, fennel & apple salad, 216, *217*
vintage apple cake, 125, *127*
apricots: soft bitter almond biscuits, *226*, 227
artichokes
artichoke salad with Parmesan, 208
braised with vermouth, 206, *207*
buying & preparing, 206, 208
rice salad, *170*, 171
types, 208
white asparagus in oil, *254*, 255
Asparagi Bianchi sott'Olio, *254*, 255
asparagus, *18–19*
spring vegetable soup, 172, *173*
white asparagus & boiled eggs, 30
white asparagus in oil, *254*, 255
aubergines: stew, 93

Baccalà alla Veneta, 84, *85*
Baccalà Mantecato, 20, *21–22*, *23*
barley, pearl: chunky vegetable & bean soup, 44, *45*
basil
pot roast with parsley sauce, 198, *199*
small potato dumplings with basil pesto, 174–76
stir-fried fine beans with basil & garlic, *210*, 211
tomato sauce with basil & garlic, 256–57, *258*
tomatoes with garlic &, 95
beans *see* borlotti beans; broad beans; green beans
beef
deep-fried shredded beef rissoles, 144–45
meatballs in tomato sauce, 202, *203*
pot roast with parsley sauce, 198, *199*
slow-cooked beef stew, 197
Bigoi col Ragù de Anara, 63–64, *65*
Bigoi in Salsa, *66*, 67
Bisato in Umido, 80–81
biscuits *see* cakes & biscuits
Bisi col Pomodoro, 92
Bollito di Manzo e Salsa Verde, 198, *199*
borlotti beans, 88–89
bean & pasta soup, *46*, *47–48*
chunky vegetable & bean soup, 44, *45*
creamed borlotti beans, *102*, 103
& radicchio, 98, *99*
& tomato salad, 212, *213*
Branzino al Cartoccio, 188, *189*
bream: baked gilthead bream with potatoes, *186*, 187
broad beans: spring vegetable soup, 172, *173*
Brusaoci in Paea co la Panseta, 90, *91*

cabbage: braised, 100
cakes & biscuits
almond polenta shortbread tart, *118*, 119
crumbly Easter teacake, 115–16, *117*
polenta cake with dried fruit, 120, *121*
polenta olive oil cake with rosemary & lemon, 234–35, *236*
polenta raisin biscuits, 111
rice pudding tartlets, *112*, 113–14
ricotta pudding cake, 241, *242*, *243*
soft bitter almond biscuits, *224–5*, *226*, 227
Venetian-style doughnuts, *122*, 123–24
vintage apple cake, 125, *127*
Calamari Ripieni, 194, *195–96*
Capelonghe con Aglio e Prezzemolo, 154, *155*
Capesante Gratinate con Mandorle e Arancia, *152*, 153
Carciofi al Vermouth, 206, *207*
carrots
chunky vegetable & bean soup, 44, *45*
pickled vegetable medley, 260, *261*
spring vegetable soup, 172, *173*
cauliflower: pickled vegetable medley, 260, *261*
celery
baby octopus & potato salad, *190*, 191–92
chunky vegetable & bean soup, 44, *45*
pickled vegetable medley, 260, *261*
spring vegetable soup, 172, *173*
charcuterie *see* pork
chard: sautéed leafy greens with pine nuts & raisins, 209
cheese
artichoke salad with Parmesan, 208
frittata with wild herbs, 31

polenta with wild mushrooms & Grana, *38*, *39*
rice salad, *170*, 171
cherries: grappa-soaked, 268, *269*
chestnuts: roasted, 40, *41*
chicken
    chicken liver risotto, 58–59
    gallina padovana breed, 200
    hen in red wine, 200–201
    in red sauce, 70, *71*
chicory: sautéed leafy greens with pine nuts & raisins, 209
cicchetti
    deep-fried cod rissoles, 146, *147*
    deep-fried shredded beef rissoles, 144–45
    hard-boiled eggs with anchovies, 142, *143*
    see also crostini
Ciliegie alla Grappa, 268, *269*
Cipolline sott'Aceto, 265
clams
    linguine with clams & lemon, 161, *162*
    razor clams with garlic & parsley, 154, *155*
cod
    deep-fried cod rissoles, 146, *147*
    dried cod mousse, *20*, 21–22, *23*
    stockfish stew, 84, *85*
coffee
    ice cream 'drowned' in coffee & amaretto, 228, *229*
    tiramisù, 'pick me up' pudding, *108*, 109–10
Conejo in Tecia, 74, *75*
cornmeal *see* polenta
Coste, Spinaci e Catalogna con Pinoli e Uvetta, 209
courgettes: marinated, *214*, 215
cream: tiramisù, 'pick me up' pudding, *108*, 109–10
Crostata di Patate Americane, 238–40, *239*
crostini
    dried cod mousse, *20*, 21–22, *23*
    grilled polenta 'crostini' with *lardo*, 36, *37*
    mackerel & pickled onion, 141
Crostini con Sgombro e Cipolline, 141

Crostini de Poenta col Lardo, 36, *37*
cucumber: pickled vegetable medley, 260, *261*
cuttlefish
    black cuttlefish stew, *86*, 87
    with peas, 87

dandelions: stir-fried leaves with pancetta, 90, *91*
desserts *see* puddings & desserts
doughnuts: Venetian-style, *122*, 123–24
drinks
    lemon sorbet with prosecco & grappa, 247
    spritz, Padua-style, 138, *139*
duck
    bigoli with duck ragù, 63–64, *65*
    stock, 64

eel
    braised, 80–81
    chargrilled, 81
eggs
    frittata with wild herbs, 31
    hard-boiled with anchovies, 142, *143*
    rice salad, *170*, 171
    white asparagus & boiled, 30

Fagiolini Aglio e Basilico, *210*, 211
Faraona Rosta, 72
Fasoi Schiceti, *102*, 103
fennel
    braised in milk, 222–23
    choosing, 223
    radicchio, fennel & apple salad, 216, *217*
Fichi Secchi, 274–76, *275*
figs
    dried, 274–76, *275*
    green fig vanilla jam, 271–73, *272*
    polenta cake with dried fruit, 120, *121*
    prosciutto &, *148*, 149
Finocchi al Latte, 222–23
fish & shellfish
    baby octopus & potato salad, *190*, 191–92
    baked gilthead bream with potatoes, *186*, 187

    baking whole, 187
    bigoli with anchovies & onions, *66*, 67
    black cuttlefish stew, *86*, 87
    braised eel, 80–81
    cuttlefish with peas, 87
    deep-fried cod rissoles, 146, *147*
    dried cod mousse, *20*, 21–22, *23*
    fried grey shrimp, *24*, 25–26
    fried marinated sardines with onions, 27–28, *29*
    hard-boiled eggs with anchovies, 142, *143*
    linguine with clams & lemon, 161, *162*
    mackerel & pickled onion crostini, 141
    mixed fried fish, *82*, 83
    poached mackerel with aromatics, 184, *185*
    prawn & prosecco risotto, 158–60, *159*
    razor clams with garlic & parsley, 154, *155*
    rice salad, *170*, 171
    scallop gratin with almonds & orange, *152*, 153
    sea bass parcels, 188, *189*
    spaghetti with scampi, 164–65, *167*
    stockfish stew, 84, *85*
    stuffed squid, *194*, 195–96
Folpetti e Patate, *190*, 191–92
Fritaja de Erbe, 31
Fritole, *122*, 123–24
Fritto Misto, *82*, 83
fruit
    baked peaches with mascarpone cream, *230*, 231
    candied quince paste, 277
    grape must pudding, 128, *129*
    grappa-soaked cherries, 268, *269*
    green fig vanilla jam, 271–73, *272*
    lemon sorbet with prosecco & grappa, 247
    peaches in syrup, 270
    polenta olive oil cake with rosemary & lemon, 234–35, *236*
    prosciutto & figs, *148*, 149
    radicchio, fennel & apple salad, 216, *217*

raspberries with rosé wine, 232, *233*
soft bitter almond biscuits, 224–25, *226*, 227
vintage apple cake, 125, *127*
fruit, dried
    dried figs, 272–74, *273*
    fried marinated pumpkin with onion, pine nuts & raisins, 150, *151*
    polenta cake with dried fruit, 120, *121*
    polenta raisin biscuits, 111
    sautéed leafy greens with pine nuts & raisins, 209
    Venetian-style doughnuts, *122*, 123–24
Fugassa de Pomi, 125, *127*

Gallina Ubriaca, 200–201
game
    bigoli with duck ragù, 63–64, *65*
    pan-roasted rabbit, 74, *75*
    tagliatelle with rabbit ragù, *60*, 61–62
garlic
    mashed potatoes with rosemary &, 101
    razor clams with garlic & parsley, 154, *155*
    stir-fried fine beans with basil &, *210*, 211
    tomato sauce with basil &, 256–57, *258*
    tomatoes with garlic & basil, 95
Giardiniera, 260, *261*
    uses, 171
Gnocchetti al Pesto, 174–76
Gnocchi, 156–57
    pumpkin gnocchi with sage butter & walnuts, 177–79, *178*
    small potato dumplings with basil pesto, 174–76
Gnocchi di Zucca al Burro e Noci, 177–79, *178*
grapes: grape must pudding, 128, *129*
grappa
    grappa-soaked cherries, 268, *269*
    lemon sorbet with prosecco &, 247
    polenta raisin biscuits, 111
    Venetian-style doughnuts, *122*, 123–24

green beans
    pickled vegetable medley, 260, *261*
    spring vegetable soup, 172, *173*
    stir-fried fine beans with basil & garlic, *210*, 211
Grigliata, 76–77
guinea fowl: roast, 72

ham *see* pork
herbs
    beef pot roast with parsley sauce, 198, *199*
    frittata with wild, 31
    mashed potatoes with rosemary & garlic, 101
    polenta olive oil cake with rosemary & lemon, 234–35, *236*
    pumpkin gnocchi with sage butter & walnuts, 177–79, *178*
    razor clams with garlic & parsley, 154, *155*
    small potato dumplings with basil pesto, 174–76
    stir-fried fine beans with basil & garlic, *210*, 211
    tomato sauce with basil & garlic, 256–57, *258*
    tomatoes with garlic & basil, 95
    see also vegetables
hops: wild hop risotto, 49–52, *50, 51*

ice cream: 'drowned' in coffee & amaretto, 228, *229*
Insalata d'Autunno, 216, *217*
Insalata di Borlotti e Pomodori, 212, *213*
Insalata di Carciofi e Parmigiano, 208
Insalata di Riso, *170*, 171

jam: green fig vanilla, 271–73, *272*

Lamponi al Vino, 232, *233*
langoustines *see* scampi
lardo, 35
    bean & pasta soup, 46, *47*–48
    grilled polenta 'crostini' with, 36, *37*
Lasagne al Radicchio e Salsiccia, 180–81
lemons
    lemon sorbet with prosecco & grappa, 247
    linguine with clams &, 161, *162*

polenta olive oil cake with rosemary &, 234–35, *236*
Linguine alle Vongole e Limone, 161, *162*

mackerel
    braised eel, 80–81
    & pickled onion crostini, 141
    poached with aromatics, 184, *185*
Marmellata di Fichi Verdi e Vaniglia, 271–73, *272*
Maroni Rosti, 40, *41*
mascarpone
    baked peaches with mascarpone cream, *230*, 231
    home-made, 110
    tiramisù, 'pick me up' pudding, *108*, 109–10
meat
    barbecued pork ribs, pancetta & sausage with rosemary, 76–77
    bean & pasta soup, 46, *47*–48
    beef pot roast with parsley sauce, 198, *199*
    boneless veal roast, 73
    chicken in red sauce, 70, *71*
    cured meats, *32–33*, 34–35
    deep-fried shredded beef rissoles, 144–45
    hen in red wine, 200–201
    meatballs in tomato sauce, 202, *203*
    prosciutto & figs, *148*, 149
    roast guinea fowl, 72
    slow-cooked beef stew, 197
    stir-fried dandelion leaves with pancetta, 90, *91*
    tagliatelle with rabbit ragù, *60*, 61–62
    see also game; offal
Menestra de Fasoi, 46, *47*–48
Mezzo Uovo con l'Acciuga, 142, *143*
Minestrone, 44, *45*
Minestrone Primavera, 172, *173*
mushrooms
    hen in red wine, 200–201
    polenta with wild mushrooms & Grana, *38*, 39

nuts
    almond polenta shortbread tart, *118*, 119

fried marinated pumpkin with onion, pine nuts & raisins, 150, *151*

ice cream 'drowned' in coffee & amaretto, 228, *229*

polenta cake with dried fruit, 120, *121*

polenta olive oil cake with rosemary & lemon, 234–35, *236*

pumpkin gnocchi with sage butter & walnuts, 177–79, *178*

ricotta pudding cake, 241, *242, 243*

roasted chestnuts, 40, *41*

sautéed leafy greens with pine nuts & raisins, 209

scallop gratin with almonds & orange, *152*, 153

small potato dumplings with basil pesto, 174–76

soft bitter almond biscuits, 224–25, *226*, 227

Venetian-style doughnuts, *122*, 123–24

octopus

baby octopus & potato salad, *190*, 191–92

cleaning, 191

offal: chicken liver risotto, 58–59

onions

baby varieties, 104, 265

bigoli with anchovies &, *66*, 67

fried marinated pumpkin with onion, pine nuts & raisins, 150, *151*

fried marinated sardines with, 27–28, *29*

mackerel & pickled onion crostini, 141

pickled baby, 265

pickled vegetable medley, 260, *261*

sweet & sour braised baby, 104, *105*

orange blossom water: ricotta pudding cake, 241, *242, 243*

oranges: scallop gratin with almonds &, *152*, 153

Orata al Forno con le Patate, *186*, 187

Ovi e Sparasi, 30

pancetta, 35

barbecued pork ribs, pancetta & sausage with rosemary, 76–77

hen in red wine, 200–201

stir-fried dandelion leaves with, 90, *91*

parsley

beef pot roast with parsley sauce, 198, *199*

razor clams with garlic &, 154, *155*

Pasqualina, 115–16, *117*

pasta

bean & pasta soup, 46, *47*–48

bigoli with anchovies & onions, *66*, 67

bigoli with duck ragù, 63–64, *65*

linguine with clams & lemon, 161, *162*

making fresh, 62, 181

radicchio & Italian sausage lasagne, 180–81

spaghetti with fresh tomato, 168, *169*

spaghetti with scampi, 164–65, *167*

spring vegetable soup, 172, *173*

tagliatelle with rabbit ragù, *60*, 61–62

Pasta al Pomodoro, 256

Pastine de Riso, *112*, 113–14

Patate Tipo Purè, 101

peaches

baked with mascarpone cream, *230*, 231

in syrup, 270

peas

cuttlefish with, 87

in red sauce, 92

rice & pea soup, 53, *54, 55*

spring vegetable soup, 172, *173*

Peperoni Grigliati sott'Olio, *262*, 264

Peperoni in Agrodolce, 263

Peperoni in Vasetto, *262*, 263–64

peppers

aubergine stew, 93

pickled vegetable medley, 260, *261*

preserved, two ways, *262*, 263–64

Persegada o Cotognata, 277

Pesche al Forno col Mascarpone, *230*, 231

Pesche Sciroppate, 270

pesto: small potato dumplings with basil pesto, 174–76

pickles

mackerel & pickled onion crostini, 141

pickled baby onions, 265

pickled vegetable medley, 260, *261*

sweet & sour peppers, 263

pine nuts

fried marinated pumpkin with onion, pine nuts & raisins, 150, *151*

polenta cake with dried fruit, 120, *121*

sautéed leafy greens with pine nuts & raisins, 209

small potato dumplings with basil pesto, 174–76

Venetian-style doughnuts, *122*, 123–24

Pinza Veneta, 120, *121*

Poenta e Funghi, 38, 39

polenta

almond polenta shortbread tart, *118*, 119

fried grey shrimp, *24*, 25–26

grilled polenta 'crostini' with *lardo*, *36*, 37

polenta cake with dried fruit, 120, *121*

polenta olive oil cake with rosemary & lemon, 234–35, *236*

polenta raisin biscuits, 111

with wild mushrooms & Grana, *38*, 39

Pollo in Tocio, 70, *71*

Polpette al Sugo, 202, *203*

Polpette di Baccalà, 146, *147*

Polpette di Carne, 144–45

pomegranate: grilled radicchio with, 218–19, *221*

Pomodori Ajo e Basilico, 95

pork

barbecued pork ribs, pancetta & sausage with rosemary, 76–77

bean & pasta soup, 46, *47*–48

cured meats, *32–33*, 34–35

hen in red wine, 200–201

meatballs in tomato sauce, 202, *203*

prosciutto & figs, *148*, 149

radicchio & Italian sausage lasagne, 180–81

stir-fried dandelion leaves with pancetta, 90, *91*

potatoes

baby octopus & potato salad, *190*, 191–92

baked gilthead bream with, *186*, 187

mashed with rosemary & garlic, 101

small potato dumplings with basil pesto, 174–76

prawns

mixed fried fish, *82*, 83

& prosecco risotto, 158–60, *159*

prosciutto, 35

& figs, *148*, 149

Prosciutto e Fichi, *148*, 149

prosecco

lemon sorbet with prosecco & grappa, 247

prawn & prosecco risotto, 158–60, *159*

puddings & desserts

almond polenta shortbread tart, *118*, 119

baked peaches with mascarpone cream, *230*, 231

candied quince paste, 277

grape must pudding, 128, *129*

grappa-soaked cherries, 268, *269*

ice cream 'drowned' in coffee & amaretto, 228, *229*

lemon sorbet with prosecco & grappa, 247

peaches in syrup, 270

raspberries with rosé wine, 232, *233*

rice pudding tartlets, *112*, 113–14

ricotta pudding cake, 241, *242, 243*

sweet potato tart, 238–40, *239*

tiramisu, 'pick me up' pudding, *108*, 109–10

zabaglione with Muscat wine, 244–46, *245*

see also cakes and biscuits

pulses *see* borlotti beans

pumpkin

chunky vegetable & bean soup, 44, *45*

fried marinated with onion, pine nuts & raisins, 150, *151*

pumpkin gnocchi with sage butter & walnuts, 177–79, *178*

rice & pumpkin soup, 56, *57*

quinces: candied quince paste, 277

rabbit

lessening 'wild' flavour, 74

pan-roasted, 74, *75*

tagliatelle with rabbit ragù, 60, 61–62

radicchio

borlotti beans &, 98, *99*

grilled with pomegranate, 218–19, *221*

& Italian sausage lasagne, 180–81

radicchio, fennel & apple salad, 216, *217*

types, 180, 181, 216

Radicchio Grigliato al Melograno, 218–19, *221*

Radeci e Fasoi, 98, *99*

raisins

fried marinated pumpkin with onion, pine nuts &, 150, *151*

polenta cake with dried fruit, 120, *121*

polenta raisin biscuits, 111

sautéed leafy greens with pine nuts &, 209

Venetian-style doughnuts, *122*, 123–24

raspberries: with rosé wine, 232, *233*

rice

chicken liver risotto, 58–59

& pea soup, 53, *54, 55*

prawn & prosecco risotto, 158–60, *159*

& pumpkin soup, 56, *57*

rice pudding tartlets, *112*, 113–14

rice salad, *170*, 171

wild hop risotto, 49–52, *50, 51*

ricotta: ricotta pudding cake, 241, *242, 243*

Risi e Bisi, 53, *54, 55*

Risi e Suca, 56, *57*

Risotto de Fegadini, 58–59

Risotto de Bruscandoli, 49–52, *50, 51*

Risotto Gamberi e Prosecco, 158–60, *159*

rissoles

deep-fried cod rissoles, 146, *147*

deep-fried shredded beef rissoles, 144–45

Rodolo de Vedeo, 73

rosemary

mashed potatoes with rosemary & garlic, 101

polenta olive oil cake with rosemary & lemon, 234–35, *236*

sage: pumpkin gnocchi with sage butter & walnuts, 177–79, *178*

salads

artichoke with Parmesan, 208

baby octopus & potato, *190*, 191–92

borlotti beans & radicchio, 98, *99*

borlotti beans & tomato, 212, *213*

radicchio, fennel & apple, 216, *217*

rice, *170*, 171

tomatoes with garlic & basil, 95

salame, 35

Salsa de Meansane, 93

salsa verde, 198, *199*

Sarde in Saor, 27–28, *29*

sardines

bigoli with anchovies & onions, 66, 67

fried marinated sardines with onions, 27–28, *29*

sausage

barbecued pork ribs, pancetta & sausage with rosemary, 76–77

radicchio & Italian sausage lasagne, 180–81

Sbrisolona, *118*, 119

scallops

gratin with almonds & orange, *152*, 153

mixed fried fish, *82*, 83

scampi: spaghetti with scampi, 164–65, *167*

Schie Frite, 24, *25*–26

sea bass

baked gilthead bream with potatoes, *186*, 187

parcels, 188, *189*

Segolete in Dolsegarbo, 104, *105*

Sepe al Nero, 86, 87
Seppie coi Piselli, 87
Sgombro agli Odori, 184, *185*
Sgroppino, 247
shellfish *see* fish & shellfish
shrimp: fried grey, *24*, 25–26
sopressa, 35
sorbet: lemon with prosecco &
  grappa, 247
soups
  bean & pasta, *46*, 47–48
  chunky vegetable & bean, 44, *45*
  rice & pea, 53, *54, 55*
  rice & pumpkin, 56, *57*
  spring vegetable, 172, *173*
Spaghetti alla Busara, 164–65, *167*
Spaghetti col Pomodoro Fresco, 168, *169*
Spezzatino, 197
spinach: sautéed leafy greens with pine
  nuts & raisins, 209
Spritz al Cynar, 138, *139*
squid
  mixed fried fish, *82*, 83
  stuffed, *194*, 195–96
stews
  aubergine, 93
  black cuttlefish, *86*, 87
  slow-cooked beef, 197
  stockfish, 84, *85*
stockfish
  dried cod mousse, *20*, *21–22, 23*
  stew, 84, *85*
Sugo di Pomodoro, 256–57, *258*
Sùgoi, 128, *129*
sweet potato tart, 238–40, *239*

Taiadele col Conejo, 60, *61–62*
tarts
  almond polenta shortbread,
    118, 119
  rice pudding, *112*, 113–14
  sweet potato, 238–40, *239*
Tiramisù, *108*, 109–10
tomatoes
  aubergine stew, 93
  borlotti beans & tomato salad,
    212, *213*
  meatballs in tomato sauce,
    202, *203*
  peeling, 165

spaghetti with fresh tomato,
  168, *169*
spaghetti with scampi, 164–65, *167*
tomato sauce with basil & garlic,
  256–57, *258*
with garlic & basil, 95
Torta di Polenta al Limone e Rosmarino,
  234–35, *236*
Torta Morbida alla Ricotta, 241, *242, 243*
tuna: rice salad, *170*, 171

veal: boneless roast, 73
vegetables
  aubergine stew, 93
  baked gilthead bream with
    potatoes, *186*, 187
  borlotti beans & radicchio, 98, *99*
  braised artichokes with vermouth,
    206, *207*
  braised cabbage, 100
  chunky vegetable & bean soup,
    44, *45*
  creamed borlotti beans, *102*, 103
  fennel braised in milk, 222–23
  fried marinated pumpkin with
    onion, pine nuts & raisins,
    150, *151*
  grilled radicchio with pomegranate,
    218–19, *221*
  marinated courgettes, *214, 215*
  mashed potatoes with rosemary
    & garlic, 101
  meatballs in tomato sauce, 202, *203*
  peas in red sauce, 92
  polenta with wild mushrooms
    & Grana, *38*, 39
  preserved peppers, two ways,
    262, 263–64
  pumpkin gnocchi with sage butter
    & walnuts, 177–79, *178*
  radicchio & Italian sausage lasagne,
    180–81
  rice & pea soup, 53, *54, 55*
  rice & pumpkin soup, 56, *57*
  sautéed leafy greens with pine nuts
    & raisins, 209
  small potato dumplings with basil
    pesto, 174–76
  spaghetti with fresh tomato,
    168, *169*

spring vegetable soup, 172, *173*
stir-fried dandelion leaves with
  pancetta, 90, *91*
stir-fried fine beans with basil &
  garlic, *210*, 211
sweet & sour braised baby onions,
  104, *105*
sweet potato tart, 238–40, *239*
tomato sauce with basil & garlic,
  256–57, *258*
white asparagus & boiled eggs, 30
white asparagus in oil, *254, 255*
wild hop risotto, 49–52, *50, 51*
see also herbs; pickles; salads
vermouth: braised artichokes with,
  206, *207*
Verze Sofegà, 100

walnuts
  polenta cake with dried fruit,
    120, *121*
  pumpkin gnocchi with sage butter
    &, 177–79, *178*
wine
  braised artichokes with vermouth,
    206, *207*
  hen in red, 200–201
  raspberries with rosé, 232, *233*
  zabaglione with Muscat,
    244–46, *245*
  see also prosecco

Zabaione al Moscato Passito,
  244–46, *245*
Zaeti, *106–7*, 111
Zucca in Saor, 150, *151*
Zucchine Marinate, *214, 215*

One of my earliest childhood memories is of sitting with my nonna *in the shade of a large magnolia tree on a hot July day, podding the peas and beans that we had harvested from the garden, and sorting the first of the tomatoes — some for salad, some for sauce.*

———

I was lucky enough to be born and raised in a little corner of the Venetian countryside, surrounded by fields, vegetable patches, and a host of seasonal, fresh food. Growing up in close proximity to my grandparents (who lived and breathed the traditional knowledge bound to the land and its rituals), as well as to the influential city of Venice, gave me the chance to absorb much of the fast-disappearing food culture that is a crucial part of the region's identity, and, eventually, to pour it all into the pages of this book.

Telling stories of food, people and places, and sharing recipes that are as delicious as they are meaningful, is what I have always wanted to do. With this in mind, I first studied for a degree in cultural studies and foreign languages, and then for a master in food studies and communication at the University of Gastronomic Sciences.

I have been working in food and with food ever since, wearing many hats but never losing sight of that initial spark. I write a food blog, Life Love Food, where I share snippets of daily life and Italian-inspired recipes, and collaborate with a number of food brands and international online and print publications. I am also a columnist for the leading Italian newspaper *Corriere della Sera*, and my work has appeared, among others, in the *Guardian*, *Die Zeit*, *Monocle*, Food52 and Design*Sponge.

———